MW01234392

PREPARE *for* WAR!

Put on the Full Armor of God

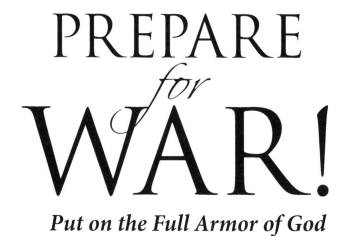

BENJAMIN H. WOODCOX

WESTBOW
PRESS*
A DIVISION OF THOMAS NELSON
& ZONDERVAN

This book is a work of non-fiction. Unless otherwise noted, the author and the publisher make no explicit guarantees as to the accuracy of the information contained in this book and in some cases, names of people and places have been altered to protect their privacy.

Scripture taken from the New King James Version®. Copyright © 1982 by Thomas Nelson. Used by permission. All rights reserved.

WestBow Press books may be ordered through booksellers or by contacting:

WestBow Press
A Division of Thomas Nelson & Zondervan
1663 Liberty Drive
Bloomington, IN 47403
www.westbowpress.com
1 (866) 928-1240

Because of the dynamic nature of the Internet, any web addresses or links contained in this book may have changed since publication and may no longer be valid. The views expressed in this work are solely those of the author and do not necessarily reflect the views of the publisher, and the publisher hereby disclaims any responsibility for them.

Any people depicted in stock imagery provided by Thinkstock are models, and such images are being used for illustrative purposes only. Certain stock imagery © Thinkstock.

ISBN: 978-1-9736-0036-7 (sc)
ISBN: 978-1-9736-0038-1 (hc)
ISBN: 978-1-9736-0037-4 (e)

Library of Congress Control Number: 2017913072

Print information available on the last page.

WestBow Press rev. date: 09/05/2017

For my friends and family.
It is my prayer you *run the race with endurance
keeping your eyes fixed firmly upon Jesus,
the author and finisher of our faith*!

Contents

Be Strong!

Be strong in the Lord and the Power of His might. Put on the whole armor of God that you may be able to stand against the wiles of the devil. Stand therefor, having girded your waist with truth [prepared for war—armed with truth—thy word is truth], having put on the breastplate of righteousness [Christ is our righteousness—stand on and for his righteousness], and having shod your feet with the preparation of the gospel of peace [proclaiming the gospel as we go!]; above all taking the shield of faith with which you will be able to quench all the fiery darts of the wicked one [soaked in the word as water—prepared and actively defending against temptation/lies/ schemes of the enemy]. And take the helmet of salvation, and the sword of the Spirit, which is the word of God; praying always with all prayer and supplication in the Spirit. (Eph. 6:10–18)

1

PREPARE FOR WAR—
BELT OF TRUTH

Ephesians 6:10–20

The morning started normal enough—pretty uneventful, actually. On top of this, it was not yet 8:00 a.m., and the temperature was already a comforting seventy-three degrees. Except for the occasional cloud, skies were clear. All in all, it was starting off to be a beautiful day. Little did those at the US naval base at Pearl Harbor know this morning was about to take a terrible turn.

At approximately 7:53 a.m. the quiet morning skies were *suddenly* pierced with the sound of fighter planes entering the air over the base. Before this surprise attack on the morning of December 7, 1941, would cease, all eight US Navy battleships housed here would be damaged, with five completely sunk, 188 US aircraft destroyed, and 2,403 Americans would lose their lives, with another 1,178 wounded. When it was all said and done, 350

1

fighter planes attacked the base over a two-hour period, catching them unprepared.[1]

Obviously, if they had known the enemy's plans, they would have been prepared, and the results would have been much different. They had the means to defend themselves against an attack, and they would have! They would not have known and just sat and let the aggressor complete their assault unchallenged. As believers in Christ, we too must keep in mind that we similarly have an opponent that would like to catch us unaware and then ill-prepared to defend against his schemes. Knowing the enemy could attack anytime, as believers we must be prepared. We must heed the call of 1 Peter 5:8 to, "Be sober, be vigilant; because your adversary the devil walks about like a roaring lion, seeking whom he *may* devour." May is a key word; we as believers have been given the armor and weapons to defend against the aggressor. We just need to put it on and be vigilant or watchful!

First and foremost, if you *are* on the side of Christ, you are on the winning side! There is a line in the book of Joel that flashes out as a stark warning. It is found in Joel 3:9, and it is a directive really toward all, though it is ultimately fulfilled and only relevant to those who do not choose Christ as Lord. It is a call for the enemies of God to prepare themselves for war. The story of Joel, though, shows us that all of the efforts by the enemy are useless and futile; those who fight against God cannot win. Nahum 1:3 declares, "The LORD *hath* his way in the whirlwind and in the storm, and the clouds *are* the dust of his feet." Even when things seem out of control and chaotic, we know God has all things under control! And while in Christ we are on the winning side, we too must prepare for war, as the enemy will

---

[1] "World War II" Timeline. The History Place. 1997. http://www. historyplace.com/worldwar2/timeline/pearl.htm

not leave us unchallenged. The enemy will engage us in a battle. Two areas need to be addressed in this battle: First, we need to consider the spiritual aspect. Ephesians 6:12 tells us, "For we do not wrestle against flesh and blood, but against principalities, against powers, against the rulers of the darkness of this age, against spiritual hosts of wickedness in heavenly places." Believers have a real spiritual enemy known as Satan, whose desire is to see you fall. John 10:10 says the enemy comes but to kill, steal, and destroy. This enemy has been around for a very long time and is very cunning, and he knows human nature and is good at setting traps for you. So while the battle is spiritual, the second area that needs to be addressed is our flesh.

The enemy uses our internal physical weaknesses to try to cause us to fall. As Galatians 5:17 lets us know, internally we have this flesh that wars against the Spirit. Additionally, Mark 7:21–23 declares, "For from within, out of the heart of men, proceed evil thoughts, adulteries, fornications, murders, Thefts, covetousness, wickedness, deceit, lasciviousness, an evil eye, blasphemy, pride, foolishness: All these evil things come from within, and defile the man." It is these lusts of the flesh the enemy uses against us in his spiritual attacks. He schemes to try to bring destruction into your life, be it through debt, drugs, alcohol, lust, negativity, lying, or stealing—however he can get to you. And if he can fight you on your terms and in your strength, he will win. Having said all this …

We Prepare for War!

Scripture not only tells us we need to prepare but also how to prepare! Ephesians 6:10 instructs us, "Be strong in the Lord, and in the power of his might." Then we are told *how* to obtain His might in verse 11:

by putting on the whole armor of God. *And* He gives us His Holy Spirit to make it all possible! It is in following the instructions in Ephesians 6 that we put on the strength of God. In being armed with *His power,* we are guaranteed victory—for He has already won the battle for us. God knows what it takes to defeat the enemy. He has given us all the necessary instructions so that we might overcome the enemy and to then live a victorious life. In Him, we truly are more than conquerors; we need only to walk in the victory of Christ!

The following scripture set says a whole lot about God's ability and then ours in Him. Colossians 1:10–17 declares:

> That ye might walk worthy of the Lord unto all pleasing, being fruitful in every good work, and *increasing in the knowledge of God; Strengthened with all might, according to his glorious power,* unto all patience and longsuffering with joyfulness; Giving thanks unto the Father, which hath made us meet to be partakers of the inheritance of the saints in light: Who hath *delivered us from the power of darkness,* and hath translated us into the kingdom of his dear Son: In whom we have redemption through his blood, even the forgiveness of sins: Who is the image of the invisible God, the firstborn of every creature: For by him were all things created, that are in heaven, and that are in earth, visible and invisible, whether they be thrones, or dominions, or principalities, or powers: all things were created by him, and for him: And he is before all things, and by him all things consist.

This scripture set says a lot about the power of God at work in the lives of believers as they learn about Him and walk in His ways. We are told we were delivered (past tense) from the power of darkness by a God over every other power. Honestly, if we believe what this says about God and what He has done for us, we should be walking victoriously. The battle begins in the mind by understanding this and then accepting nothing less as we draw near to God, learn His ways, and then walk in them!

This Is How We Overcome!

As we progress, we will speak more about how the word of God helps us to break down strongholds which keep us from having our minds renewed and often times prevents us from living the life that is available in Christ. We must have an understanding of God's ways and then commit ourselves to allow His thoughts be our thoughts and be obedient to walk in them. A key passage to keep in mind is John 8:31–32, in which Jesus told the Jews who believed on Him *if* they abide in His word, they are His disciples indeed and they shall know the truth, and the truth shall set them free! The big *if* here is *if* they abide in His word. If we want the life Christ died for us to have, we are going to have to know Him as our personal Savior. And as such, *He must become our greatest treasure in life!* We are not going to get it through a lukewarm faith!

> This know also, that in the last days perilous times shall come. For men shall be lovers of their own selves, covetous, boasters, proud, blasphemers, disobedient to parents, unthankful, unholy, Without natural affection, trucebreakers, false accusers, incontinent, fierce, despisers of those that are good, Traitors, heady, highminded, lovers of pleasures more than lovers of God; Having a form of godliness, but *denying the power* thereof: from such turn away. (2 Tim. 3:1–3)

This set of scripture describes how the gospel might impact (or not) some professed believers. It has no effect on them to change them to be Christlike. But we are to be as verses 16–17 of 2 Timothy 3 declares in acknowledging, "All scripture is inspired of God and is profitable for reproof, for doctrine, for training in righteousness that the man of God may be complete thoroughly equipped toward every good work." Yes, we are to let the word of God make us complete thoroughly equipped for every good work! The first group denied the power of God to change them. We must put on the power of God. We must put on His armor! The analogy of putting the armor on our outside as a covering is truly a metaphor for the internal change taking place in us. This is how we overcome!

We Must Be Armed with Truth

Second Corinthians 10 tells us our weapons in God are mighty for the pulling down of strongholds. These strongholds are lies we believe or things we see as a truth that in God's reality are not. And we let these issues affect our lives. The first piece of armor listed is the belt of truth. It is so important for believers to be rooted/built up in truth. I once heard a pastor say the truth spoken of here is basically trueness to God. So many people neglect this area. In fact, when we are putting on the belt of truth, we are putting on Christ. Jesus said of Himself in John 14:6, "I am the way, the *truth*, and the life. No one comes to the Father except through me." Then when praying for His disciples, we read in John 17:17 He prayed they would be "sanctified in thy truth, thy *word* is truth." *You **cannot** put on the belt of truth/ Christ separate from the word.*

There's newness in Christ—a new life, new opportunity to think

6

and live differently. In speaking of the eternal sense in Revelation 21:6, Jesus states, "Behold I make *all* things new." That newness means eventually being complete, with no more tears, no more pain! But until we are reunited with Christ, we have an opportunity to expect different things than the world expects, to see things different than the world does, and to walk in the light as Christ is in the light. We have the truth of Christ and His word for this reason—the belt of truth.

For a Roman soldier, the belt girded on all the other pieces of armor. It held everything else in place. The belt held the sword. We need this truth to hold us steadfast in the faith. If we are not armed with the truth, we are unprepared!

Finally!

At the end of his writing to the church at Ephesus, Paul's exhortation to them is *finally* (v.10). In Ephesians, he reminds them of what they received in Christ, how they were saved by grace, and how they are then to walk differently. He tells them to consider everything Christ has done for them and given them the ability to do. Finally then they must be strong in the Lord, for it is in this that you will have success.

And this *finally* is not an idle acknowledgment but a statement to have understanding and then go! Trusting in the Lord—to not wane in your faith, to not backslide, to not give up, or to give in, but ever moving forward in your faith.

If you remember back to Exodus when the Israelites were slaves in Egypt, God told Pharaoh that he wanted his people freed so they could worship Him. This is still the call today for believers who have been freed to live a life of worship to God. Many are hindered in their walk with the Lord, and knowing the truth and being armed with the armor of God can set those captive free.

In Exodus 14 we further read about the Israelites coming to the Red Sea. In these passages, they have the sea in front of them—seemingly impassible—and the enemy approaching from behind. At this point, they weren't worshiping God very well. Paralyzed in fear, they were looking back to their old lives; they were letting the enemy frustrate them. They became distracted by their flesh. They forgot that God had set them free because He loved them --and because of that love would not forsake them. They let a stronghold dictate their reality instead of holding on to the promise of God.

In Exodus 14:13–14 we read Moses said to the people, "Do not be afraid. Stand still, and see the salvation of the Lord, which He will accomplish for you today. For the Egyptians whom you see today, you shall see again no more forever. The Lord will fight for you, and you shall hold your peace." God promised them the victory, and God *cannot* lose! Moses went to God, and God told Moses to stop crying to Him and move forward (v. 15). And we know the story. The sea parted, and the people crossed on dry land! God has freed you to worship Him, and when the enemy brings something our way, the same message applies for us today—go forward! Do not let the enemy cause you to look back, to turn back, and to get your eyes off the Lord! When the people went forward, they saw the salvation, the deliverance of God! To put on the armor and go forward is the call to the church today! Jesus has already been victorious, and in Him we are truly **more** than conquerors.

> *Considering all you have in Christ,*
> *finally be strong in the Lord!*

Review/Application

1. Main Point(s): List what stood out to you:

2. What did you learn about:

   - yourself/human nature:

   - the enemy:

   - God:

3. What key scriptures that spoke to you and why?

4. How can you *practically* apply the principles in this chapter to your life?

2

TIME TO TAKE A STAND!—
PROTECTED BY THE
BREASTPLATE

Ephesians 6:14

I guess we always face a culture war. But at times, it seems like the battle to sway the overall course of a society is fiercer than others. As I write this, we appear to be in one of those fiercer times. You have two very different and opposing worldviews vying to be dominant: conservatism vs. liberalism. Likewise, for a Christian, there is a battle to daily chose for what or whom we live. As we have already discussed, we have the flesh and a very real spiritual enemy vying to dominate our lives versus living by the Spirit of God in righteousness. We have to decide day by day and even minute by minute how we are going to live and ultimately for who and what purpose.

Four times we are called to stand as believers in Ephesians 6. It is time for many more to not only make a decision for Christ but to decide to stand for what honors Christ. It is time for believers everywhere to stand on the word of God and accept no less than what

Christ died for us to be, have, and do. It is time for some to arise and to no longer have a form of godliness and deny the power of God to change them but to humble themselves under the sight of God and resist the enemy. Now is the time to stand, church, and raise up a banner—the banner of truth and righteousness in our lives!

To do this, we need to put on the belt of truth, and we need to put on the breastplate of righteousness. As we spoke about last, God knows what it takes to defeat the enemy of our souls, and we need to heed the instructions He is giving us. And if we do, we will have done everything to stand.

What Is Righteousness?

Previously, we answered the question of what truth is being spoken of in the belt of truth. So as we talk about the breastplate of righteousness, we address the question, "What is the righteousness Paul is speaking about in Ephesians 6?" Pastor John MacArthur says the Bible speaks of three types,[2] the first being self-righteousness. We can be certain Paul is not talking about putting on self-righteousness. Isaiah 64:6 states, "But we are all like an unclean thing, and all our righteousness are like filthy rags; we all fade as a leaf, and our iniquities, like the wind, have taken us away." Our righteousness (or rather lack thereof) needs to be taken care of for us to have the breastplate of righteousness. We do this when we come to Christ as our Savior. We can't arm ourselves with the armor or the power of God without a relationship with Him through Christ. And when we receive Christ

---

[2] MacArthur, John. "The Armor of God: The Breastplate of Righteousness." Sermon Audio. 1/14/2014. http://www.sermonaudio.com/sermoninfo. asp?SID=11414126418

as Savior, scripture tells us Christ robes us in His righteousness, and it is this righteousness (Christ's) that MacArthur identifies as the second type of righteousness scripture identifies. But it is a third kind of righteousness MacArthur says Paul is speaking more directly about in Ephesians 6. This third type of righteousness is what MacArthur calls practical righteousness.[3] And while this flows from the righteousness of Christ imparted to us, Paul, in referring to putting on the breastplate of righteousness more specifically, is talking about being in practice what we are in position. We are in effect putting on the breastplate of righteousness when we learn and then live like Christ. And throughout scripture, this is the call of the church.

First Corinthians 15:34 tells us to "awake to righteousness, and *do not* sin." Ephesians 5:8–9 declares, "For you were once darkness, but now you are light in the Lord. Walk as children of light (for the fruit of the Spirit is in all goodness, righteousness, and truth)." Verse 14 goes on to call the believer to "awake ye who sleep, arise from the dead and Christ will give you light." There are many in the church who need to awaken! Awake, church! You once were darkness. Now you are light. Walk as children of light. Put on Christ. Put on the breastplate of righteousness!

In the King James Version of the Bible, there are over three hundred references to righteousness in the NT, and all who had it had it not only because they knew God's ways but because they also walked in them.[4] It is by the Spirit and living by the Spirit that we are righteous. Scripture tells us we are to discipline ourselves toward godliness or righteousness. And 2 Timothy 3 says—as we

---

[3] Ibid.
[4] Ibid.

13

noted previously—that scripture is given by inspiration of God and is profitable for doctrine, for reproof, for correction, and for training in righteousness, and that the man of God may be complete, thoroughly equipped for every good work. Yes, righteousness is trained by God as we are committed to Him and taught and led by His Holy Spirit. We don't have to learn everything the hard way from experience. We can learn from God and walk in His ways and experience life differently. Dr. Martyn Lloyd-Jones said, "Thank God for experiences, but do not rely on them. You do not put on the breastplate of experiences', you put on the breastplate of righteousness."[5] We do not have to learn everything from our experience, but we can learn from God's word and from how those before us fell at times and triumphed at times.

Wearing the breastplate of righteousness is being in practice what we are in position and profession. It is a lifestyle of putting into practice what we believe in our hearts. Simply put, to be righteous is to do what is right in the sight of God and we learn this from His word.

Putting on the Breastplate

Jerry Bridges in *The Pursuit of Holiness* states, "We are to flee temptation and take positive steps to avoid it … God expects us to assume our responsibilities for keeping the sinful desires of the body under control."[6] Proverbs 27:12 says, "The prudent see danger and take refuge, but the simple keep going and suffer for it." As Jerry reminds us doing this starts with changing the way we think—growing in

---

[5] Lloyd-Jones, Dr. Martin. "The Breastplate of Righteousness." MLJ Trust. https://www.mljtrust.org/search/?q=breastplate
[6] Jerry Bridges, *The Pursuit of Holiness* (Carol Stream, IL: Navpress, 1996).

our knowledge of Christ and taking every thought captive. And frankly, we must do better at this than we often do. Think you are doing pretty well at this? Maybe you are. But as Jerry addresses, if we were able to flash on a screen all of your thoughts from the past week, you would likely have to leave town. We must realize that our thought lives ultimately determine who we are—our character. King Solomon said, "For as he thinks within himself, so he is" (Proverbs 23:7). In putting on the armor and breastplate of righteousness, we become the people God has planned us to be.

A Recipe for Change

In Romans 12:1–2, we see a four-ingredient recipe for this change. These verses state:

> I beseech you therefore, brethren, by the mercies of God, that you present your bodies a living sacrifice, holy, acceptable to God, which is your reasonable service. And do not be conformed to this world, but be transformed by the renewing of your mind, that you may prove what is that good and acceptable and perfect will of God.

First, we are to *present ourselves* to God. In doing this, we are saying, "Here I am, God. You saved me. Use me for Your glory." Second, we are to *no longer conform to the ways of the world*. This is agreeing with God and committing our ways to God's ways over our own. Third, we have our *minds transformed* in learning the way God thinks and what He says is truth by His word. And fourth, we *prove it* by just doing it, living it—being in practice what we are in profession! Bridges also goes on to state, "It is obvious from even a casual reading of Proverbs 2:1–2 that the protective influence of the word of God comes as a result of diligent, prayerful, and purposeful intake of scripture. To guard our minds, we must give priority to the Bible in our lives."[7] In doing this altogether, we put on the breastplate of righteousness!

An item to note about the Roman soldier's breastplate is that it covered the soldier from neck to waist. There could be no gaps, and they definitely would not go into battle without it. To do so would be death. A gap would give room for an arrow to strike. We see a great example of this in 1 Kings 22:31-35 when evil King Ahab had an arrow strike between the scales in his armor during battle. A small crack in this evil king's armor took his life. We must not have any cracks in our armor! The cracks in our armor would be areas of sin or iniquity we knowingly commit. When the enemy brings a trap for us—a scheme—as we spoke about last previously and we give in instead of standing. The breastplate of righteousness protects us from the schemes of the enemy. I wish I could tell you it was always going to be easy to resist the flesh and temptations or schemes of the enemy. This is why we are called to resist the enemy. It takes effort at times. *But …* God gave us the Holy Spirit so we can succeed. The same Spirit that raised Christ from the dead lives in believers, guaranteeing them the victory as they press in and press on!

Time to Stand

Consider Joseph. In Genesis 39, we see his master's (Potiphar) wife try to tempt Joseph. And because of his reaction, I personally believe he was likely tempted. But Joseph's response was, "How could I do

---

[7] Ibid.

this against my master and more importantly how could I do this great wickedness and sin against God (v. 9)?" Joseph's reaction was to flee. Joseph was not going to let the flesh or this trap of the enemy keep him from living a God-honoring life. This must be the heart and attitude in us. When it is not, we expose ourselves—we create an opening in our armor. First Corinthians 10 reminds us to commit ourselves to God and rely on His might. Verses 12–14 state:

> Therefore let him who thinks he stands take heed lest he fall [can't do it on our own] no temptation has overtaken you except such as is common to man; but God is faithful, who will *not* allow you to be tempted beyond what you are able [He will empower you through the Holy Spirit as you commit your ways to Him ... hard at first, yes], but with the temptation will also make the way of escape, that you may be able to bear [beat] it. Therefore, my beloved, flee from idolatry.[8]

Joseph knew what was honoring to God and what would not have been. Despite how his flesh might or might not have felt, Joseph took a stand for God. He was *committed* to God. It wasn't easy, and he paid the price in the short run for it. But in the long run, he was the better off for it, and God was able to use him to help others and to bring God glory. For what purpose are you living? Maybe it's time to take a stand in some areas.

Take a stand! Take a stand

- against the flesh,
- against the enemy, and
- *for God!*

---

[8] Emphasis added.

Review/Application

1. Main Point(s): List what stood out to you:

2. What did you learn about:

    - yourself/human nature:

    - the enemy:

    - God:

3. What are key scriptures that spoke to you and why?

4. How can you *practically* apply the principles in this chapter to your life?

3

GOSPEL OF PEACE

"Peace I leave with you, my peace I give to you; not as the world gives do I give to you. Let not your heart be troubled, neither let it be afraid" (John 14:27). I think these encouraging words of Jesus capture the essence what the apostle Paul was trying to get through to us in Ephesians 6:15 when speaking of having our feet shod with the preparation of the gospel of peace. As I was working on this writing, I received a message asking if I could meet with a young man who was suffering. Just ending a relationship and struggling with alcohol (and due to this struggling in almost every other area of his life), he found himself with no peace. In fact, I was told he was thinking about ending his life. I was told he is not a religious person and, in fact, had no beliefs. I agreed to meet with him, knowing, whether he received the message of Christ or not, Christ was the very message that could bring peace to his life! A peace the world cannot offer - eternally lasting peace with God.

I believe having our feet shod with the preparation of the gospel, in fact, is the source for believers to have continual comfort, solace, rest, and peace in this world despite their circumstances. It is what gives them the strength to stand and persevere against the attacks or schemes of the enemy. For these reasons, it is this important piece of armor that we need to have a better understanding of than we often do.

Your God Reigns!

After a quick review of the meaning behind the phrase, "Having shod your feet with the preparation of the gospel of peace," you will quickly find there are a couple of different camps as to what specifically Paul is referring. One group says this speaks directly about evangelism. It talks to believers about preparing to take the gospel message out and that the gospel message itself wins the fight over darkness as it illuminates darkened hearts to the truth of the gospel. Others state this is not about evangelism but simply about having our feet protected during spiritual battle – rather being prepared to stand firm in the gospel message or the peace you obtained therein with God when the enemy attacks. While I believe one of these views is more predominantly what Paul is referring to, I think the real meaning can be found to contain both areas.

First, let's start with the basics that include both the symbolism of the shoes or armor the soldier would wear and then look at the context as a whole. Soldiers would of course not consider going into battle without proper foot covering. But more than having coverage to protect on various terrain, they often had short spikes on the bottom to help with traction or for them to stand firm as they needed. Once we receive the gospel in our lives, we are to stand strong in the Lord—to shod our feet with the preparation of the gospel.

Notice we shod our feet with the preparation. We are called to be ready for an attack of the enemy. It is not if but when he attacks and to be firmly rooted and grounded in Christ. And while this is likely the primary meaning of the text, as we go, then we cannot completely separate evangelism. After all, the call to shod our feet is also a call to go in Christ. And in Christ, our lives and faith are a testimony to all He has done.

So, while the helmet of salvation deals more with receiving and growing in our salvation (as we will discuss later on), our feet shod with the preparation of the gospel of peace deals more directly and primarily with persevering in our faith but also can naturally and indirectly deal with sharing the gospel. Here are a few thoughts on the topic from others,

Pastor George Muller states, "What is this preparation of the gospel of peace? It means, we are the children of God, and we are no longer at enmity with God but are at peace with Him. Our sins are forgiven in the Lord Jesus Christ. God is well pleased with us for Christ, His dear Son's sake; and we, having no longer any fear, are at peace with God."[9] He also explains because of this, "We may be able to march homewards through the rough paths of life, and even to stand in the hour of conflict."[10]

But furthermore, in Isaiah 52:7 we read:

> How beautiful upon the mountains are the feet of him who brings good news, who proclaims peace, who brings glad tidings of good things, who proclaims salvation, who says to Zion, "Your God Reigns!"

---

[9] Muller, George. "Your Feet Shod with the Preparation of the Gospel of Peace." GeorgeMuller.org. 12/19/2016. http://www.georgemuller.org/devotional/your-feet-shod-with-the-preparation-of-the-gospel-of-peace
[10] Ibid.

These words of Isaiah teacher/author D. A. Carson sees as an earlier proclamation of what the apostle Paul speaks toward when telling us to shod our feet with the preparation of the gospel of peace.

Carson has said of the gospel of peace that the "gospel of peace on our feet indicates protection from being tripped up." He also states it "indicates going forward with it... bearing witness to what Christ did to reconcile us to God."[11]

So having our feet shod with the gospel enables us in Christ to victoriously stand against all the powers of darkness. Christ has already won the battle, so, reconciled to God in Christ and empowered by the Holy Spirit, we can stand against *all* the schemes of the enemy. Since this armor is on the feet, it is indicative of going forth. And believers going forth are going to share the good news! It would be hard to completely separate the two—persevere and go forth!

If we too narrowly define having our feet shod with the readiness of the gospel of peace, we might miss considering the whole effect or change that results in the life of a believer from receiving the gospel. It not only causes them to persevere, but wherever they are, they cannot help but to share their source of strength—*Christ*.

Persevere *and* Share Your Source of Peace!

When I was working on this, I had on my mind the following account I compiled from the writings of Corrie Ten Boom regarding the plight of her and her family. In her writings, Corrie tells how she,

---

[11] D. A. Carson, "The Christian in Complete Armor." Prydain. 2/27/2015. https://prydain.wordpress.com/2015/02/27/dr-d-a-carson-the-christian-in-complete-armor-ephesians-610-20/

her parents, and her sister harbored hundreds of Jews to protect them from arrest by Nazi authorities during WWII.[12] Betrayed by a fellow Dutch citizen, they imprisoned Corrie, her sister, Betsie, and their father. Corrie's eighty-four-year-old father soon died in the Scheveningen prison, located near the Hague. Corrie and her sister Betsie remanded to the notorious Ravensbrück concentration camp, near Berlin, which was worse than any other prison they experienced. For the first two days, they had to sleep out in the open. It poured with rain, and the ground became a sea of mud. Then they were packed into a large barracks room. It had been built to house four hundred people, but there were now fourteen hundred prisoners in it. They had to sleep on straw mattresses filled with choking dust and swarming with fleas. Even the guards did not like going into the barracks room because of the fleas. Roll call was at half-past four in the morning. There were thirty-five thousand women in the camp, and if anyone was missing, they counted them all again and again, so it often went on for hours. If the prisoners did not stand up straight, the women guards beat them with riding whips. The work was extremely hard. Corrie and Betsie had to load heavy sheets of steel on to carts, push them for a certain distance, and then unload them. All the time the guards shouted at them to work faster.

They gave the prisoners a potato and some thin soup at lunchtime and some turnip soup with a piece of black bread in the evening. The inmates who were doing lighter work had no lunch at all.

The Ten Booms were put in a circumstance that seemed hopeless. How do we understand and how do we deal with such events? How could a loving God allow this? How did they, and how are we to deal

---

[12] Corrie Ten Boom, Her Story. (New York, NY: Inspirational Press, 1995).

with hard circumstances we find ourselves facing? How are we to stand when the test becomes so hard?

The Power of the Gospel of Peace!

When they first moved into the barracks room, the conditions there made the women angry and selfish. There were arguments and fights. Everyone suffered so much that they spent all their energy looking after themselves.

When Betsie noticed this, she began to pray that God would give peace to the barracks room. Very soon the atmosphere changed. The women became a little more patient with each other. They even began to make a few jokes about their troubles. In the evenings, after a hard day's work and a miserable supper, Corrie and Betsie took out the little Dutch Bible. At first, a small group gathered round to listen, and then more and more women joined them. The guards never came in to stop them because of the fleas, so Corrie and *Betsie thanked God for the fleas!*

The women came from many countries, including Poland, France, Germany, and Russia. Corrie translated the Bible from Dutch into German; someone else translated German into Polish, and so on. Under these terrible conditions, the goodness in the words of the Bible shone out brightly, and their message of God's love brought comfort. With death all around, the promise of eternal life and the glory of heaven gave the women hope for the future. One day Betsie was cruelly whipped by a guard for not working hard enough. But she did not give into hatred. She prayed for the guards as much as she prayed for the prisoners. Corrie found this tough, but somehow

Betsie seemed to have raised above all the suffering and to be living very close to God.

"Corrie," she said, "we must tell people how good God is. After the war, we must go around the world telling people. No one will be able to say that they have suffered worse than us. We can tell them how wonderful God is and how His love will fill our lives if only we will give up our hatred and bitterness."

Gradually Betsie became weaker and weaker. It was bitterly cold, for it was now November. In the end, Betsie was so ill that they admitted her to the hospital. Corrie was not allowed to visit her sister, but each day she went to look at her through one of the hospital windows. Finally, one day Betsie's bed was empty. Corrie was heartbroken. At first, she did not dare to look in the room where they placed the dead. Then another prisoner called her. There was Betsie. Yes, she was dead. But her face had changed. Instead of being full of pain and suffering as it had been, it was now beautiful, like the face of an angel!

Once again it was roll call. The women stamped their feet to keep warm. Suddenly Corrie heard her name: "Prisoner ten Boom, report after roll call." What was going to happen? Was she going to be punished? Or shot? "Father in heaven, please help me now," she prayed.

When she reported, they gave her a card stamped "*Entlassen,*" which means "Released." She was free! She could hardly believe it. She was given back her few possessions, some new clothes, and a railway pass back to Holland. After a long, hard journey, she arrived back among friends in her own country. Afterward, she learned that they had released her by mistake. A week after her release, all the women of her age in the camp were killed.

Wait upon the Lord

In that concentration camp, Corrie and Betsie were able to serve God. Their faith was tested, yet they endured and triumphed over the enemy! Through trials that could have tempted them to do otherwise, the Ten Booms remained faithful ... with their feet shod with the preparation of the gospel... they kept their hope in God.

In Isaiah 40:30–31 we read, "Even though youths shall faint and be weary, and the young men shall utterly fall, but those that wait upon the Lord shall renew their strength. They shall mount up with wings as eagles; they shall run and not be weary, they shall walk and not faint." The promises here is they *shall* mount up, run, and not faint. But this happens as those who are weary wait on the Lord. This is more than just a passive sitting and doing nothing. The word *wait* from the Hebrew *qavah* basically means to get involved with God. The word picture would be like strands that are bound[13] together in a rope. We should be this involved with God. It is in this that we have this success!

No matter what our circumstances, we live by faith, not by sight. Have you put your faith in God? Are your feet shod with the gospel? As that Great Commission calls us to, the Ten Booms shared Christ wherever they were. They saw the gospel message as most important. So though the crux of the text appears to point to be prepared to stand—we as believers always and in everything are also prepared to share the reason for our peace.

Truly, when we know what we have received in Christ, we know we have nothing to fear but always hope! It is then we can declare

---

[13] "H6960—qavah—Strong's Hebrew Lexicon (KJV)." Blue Letter Bible. Accessed 17 Jun, 2017. https://www.blueletterbible.org//lang/lexicon/lexicon.cfm?Strongs=H6960&t=KJV

Isaiah 52:7: "How beautiful upon the mountains are the feet of him who brings good news, who proclaims peace, who brings glad tidings of good things, who proclaims salvation, who says to Zion, 'Your God Reigns!'"

Review/Application

1. Main Point(s): List what stood out to you:

2.   What did you learn about:

   - yourself/human nature:

   - the enemy:

   - God:

3. What are the key scriptures that spoke to you and why?

4. How can you *practically* apply the principles in this chapter to your life?

4

SHIELD OF FAITH

Ephesians 6:16

I remember once seeing a scene from a movie where two armies were in battle. As one army approached an area where the enemy was hiding out, suddenly the air was filled with fiery darts propelled at them. They were only safe from these fiery darts because they were prepared and lifted up their shields. Those without the protection of a shield would be either severely wounded or killed. And knowing the enemy would be shooting fiery darts, we know in no way would one of those soldiers carelessly go out without a shield. To do so would be suicide. However, this is precisely what many believers do when they do not use the shield of their faith against the schemes of the enemy—and this is the reason I think there is so much tragedy in the church. By tragedy I mean those who call themselves Christians but whose lives are no different—those who are always falling victim to the enemy's schemes. In Christ, our lives should be different. We should be more than being just like the world only with a Christian title. We must let the gospel change us, and as we learn to take up the shield of faith, this happens!

In Christ, we are more than conquerors. Since Christ already won the battle, we just have to put on His armor and go! When we do, we can endure with the victory guaranteed. And let me tell you what this equates to: you can live a life truly free in Christ. You can be prepared to stand against the schemes of the enemy and live victoriously!

As reviewed earlier, to be successful in the spiritual battle, Ephesians 6:10–18 calls believers to be strong (not in their strength) in the power of God's might. We do this by putting on the whole armor of God. And in the shield, we have a piece of weaponry that promises to extinguish every fiery dart of the enemy—not 75 percent of them or 90 percent of them but 100 percent! Are you getting excited yet in understanding what God has given us? What He has done for us! So how are we to take up this shield?

Taking up God's Shield!

In Ephesians, there are traditionally six pieces of armor noted: the belt of truth, breastplate of righteousness, feet shod with the preparation of the gospel of peace, shield of faith, the helmet of salvation, and the sword of the spirit (which is the word of God). Later I will cover what I see as a seventh. Of these six, we could note that all of them stem from and are reliant upon the word of God. This shows—as we have been reviewing—the importance of this word in our life. And while each part is important and necessary, as mentioned, today we are going to look at the shield of faith and how we take this up by taking in the word.

I once read about the practice the Roman soldiers had before going into a battle of soaking their shields in water. The purpose of this was so that when the enemy did shoot fiery arrows at them, they would hit the water-soaked wood shield covered in leather and immediately be extinguished. What a great picture of how being soaked in the word of God can help us overcome anything the enemy hurls at us! We know that Ephesians 5:16 equates the word of God to water. So it is in soaking in the word that we are prepared to take up the shield of faith. But note, the soldiers couldn't just leave the shield down; they had to hold it up to intercept and extinguish the fiery darts. This is telling us our faith must be active!

In considering the shield of faith, let's consider what we mean when talking here about faith. Hebrews 11:1 says, "Now faith is the substance of things hoped for, the evidence of things not seen." The NIV says, "Now faith is being sure of what we hope for and certain of what we do not see." This means we fully believe in God and what His word says. And we can only do this because of the work of His Holy Spirit in us. Starting from salvation faith is a work of the Holy Spirit in us. And any increase of faith comes from the continued work of the Holy Spirit abiding in us, leading us into all truth. So, on top of this, this is why it is important that we keep in the word as scripture declares "faith cometh by hearing, hearing by the word of God" (Romans 10:17).

Faith involves both believing what God says in His word as truth and being faithful to what His word says. Faith is where we stop depending on or looking primarily to self (or others) for answers and direction and instead look to God. Just knowing what truth is, is only half of it. What God tells us in His word must be hoped for, embraced, and seized. Faith involves what we believe, who we trust, and what we do. In scripture, true faith in God always resulted in faithfulness to God.

Hebrews 11 is full of stories of believers who found themselves in dire circumstances and who cried out to and trusted in God, such as Noah, Abraham (who hoped against hope), and Moses, among others. Some God delivered, some experienced the miraculous, and some died in their faith. But whether delivered or whether they died, they all remained faithful to the word of God. So to take up the shield of faith we must know what we inherited in Christ and accept nothing less.

The Fiery Darts

Before looking at an example of taking up the shield, let's briefly discuss these fiery darts that we need the shield to defend ourselves against. The fiery darts are the things the enemy hurls at us to try to get us to fall, to backslide, to turn from our faith, and to sinful, lascivious living. These darts include every form of temptation or idols intended to draw us away from abiding in God's word. These fiery darts can be: others talking about us, fear or anxieties if they hold us back, discouragement, doubt, unforgiveness, covetousness, cares of the world, or evil thoughts we don't take captive. These fiery darts are anything against the standards of God in areas such as marriage. These fiery darts are anything contrary to the word of God and living the life of freedom from sin and bondage He died for us obtain.

This battle has been going on since the time of Adam and Eve. And we must take heed of this word. First Corinthians 10:12 says, "Take heed you stand, lest you fall." We must be prepared—the enemy will come against us, and the only response is to be strong in the Lord. We *must* be prepared to take up the shield of faith, so we don't fall victim to these schemes of the enemy!

Example of Caleb and Joshua

It is in faith that we quench all the fiery darts of the enemy and have rest and all the promises God has for us. We must be prepared to take up (and lift up) the shield of faith because the enemy is going to come against you with fiery darts. An excellent example of this is that of the Israelites in the desert. When God told them to scout out the Promised Land, they sent ten spies. The majority of the spies and the Israelites let their shield down, and the enemy sent a fiery dart—evil with hell's flame—of doubt, and they lost faith in God and that he would deliver the Promised Land to them. Only two of the spies—Caleb and Joshua—kept their faith. They were not looking at what they could do but what God said He could and would do. The ultimate reason why, once freed, the Israelites did not enter the Promised Land was not because they did not know what God said He could/would do but that they did not have the faith that He would do it through or for them. When we look at scripture and see a promise of God, we must believe that not only that God can do as He says but that He will for us. We must have faith we are what this word says we are, that we have in Christ what this word says we have, and that God will do through us what this word says He will as we give our lives over to Him.

Our faith is to be both something we believe and something we live. Evil says you can't trust, have, or do what God says in His word. Caleb and Joshua, on the other hand, had faith in the word of God and stood firm. Caleb and Joshua did not know how God would overcome the enemy, but they knew God could and would because He told them.

True Faith leads to Faithfulness

I read somewhere that Charles Spurgeon commented: "The Bible recognizes no faith as true faith that does not lead to obedience."[14] In fact, in the NT often the words faith, belief, and obedience are used synonymously (see John 3:16, 18, 36). So faith is simply believing and then being obedient to what God says is truth. It is going by God's word and ability over our own ability or how it looks in the natural. Most of the Israelites failed here and never entered the Promised Land. They saw the challenge of the enemy as something they could not overcome instead of looking at it as "nothing is impossible for God!" How do we approach life's challenges?

In His epistle, James talks about a living faith. He explains dead faith results in no works while one living out one's faith and firmly rooted in Christ can't help but be fruitful. It truly is a faith without boundaries—the boundaries of what we can do in the flesh are torn down by what God can do! Hebrews 11:6 tells us without faith it is impossible to please God. God takes no pleasure in us drawing back. We are to walk in the promises of His word. Our life goal should be to live in a manner pleasing to Him, as Romans 12:21 instructs. We were created to bring Him glory. And God deserves to be glorified simply for who He is! It is the life of faith that pleases Him and glorifies Him.

True faith is overcoming conquering faith. It is prepared to stand against the wiles of the enemy—ready to take up the shield of faith to extinguish the fiery darts of the enemy. Our faith is going to be tested and tried. Will it be found to be true? Are we growing in our faith? Are we building ourselves up in our most holy faith as the book

---

[14] "Quotes." Bibile.org. https://bible.org/illustration/quotes-30

of Jude directs? Building ourselves up takes being in the word as we discussed, meditating on it, and training ourselves to respond to the attacks of the enemy with faith.

A favorite scripture set of many is found in Proverbs 3:5–6, which states, "Trust in the Lord with all your heart, and lean not on your own understanding; In all your ways acknowledge Him, and He shall direct your paths." We note the trust here from the Hebrew is more than just a thought process but a trust that comes from experience. We are to trust God actively, and as we do, we will see we can trust in Him because He has never forsaken us before.

Never Give Up!

Many people have suffered for a while with some things—wounded by fiery darts they were not prepared to stand against. Let me tell you it is not too late, and you can through Christ gain freedom from those things. We must keep our confidence in Christ and rely on His might. First Corinthians 10:12–14 says:

> Therefore let him who thinks he stands take heed lest he fall. No temptation has overtaken you except such as is common to man; but God is faithful who will not allow you to be tempted beyond what you are able, but with the temptation will also make the way of escape, that you may be able to bear it. Therefore, my beloved, flee from idolatry.

In this set, we get a great tip: to flee idolatry. What are idols? Anything we set ahead of Christ. And it also encourages us in the fact that God is faithful, so we turn to Him for help. Christ then is our answer!

After covering all the faith examples in Hebrews 11, the first few verses of Hebrews 12 encourage us: "Since we are surrounded by so great a cloud of witnesses, let us lay aside every weight and the sin which so easily ensnares us, and let us run the race with endurance that I set before us, looking unto Jesus the author and finisher of our faith." Some versions read, "Let us run the race before us and never give up." This is the high calling of the gospel.

While God has good plans for you, there is an enemy that also has plans for you: to kill, steal, and destroy. We *must* take up the shield of faith to live victoriously against the enemy. To do this we have to be in Christ, we have to be in His word, and we don't win the battle only knowing what His word says but by actively trusting and abiding in His word and not accepting the lies of the accuser. This is taking up the shield. There is a difference between knowing and actively putting into practice our faith and by that taking refuge in God through faith. When the enemy throws fiery darts, choose instead to believe God! Consider your thoughts and what you chose to think on and accept. How do they align with what God's word says? If they don't, you may need to raise the shield of faith. You may need to put into action another piece of the armor.

> Everyone born of God overcomes the world. This is the
> victory that overcomes the world, even our faith. (1 John 5:4)

Amen.

Review/Application

1. Main Point(s): List what stood out to you:

2. What did you learn about:

    - yourself/human nature:

    - the enemy:

    - God:

3. What are the key scriptures that spoke to you and why?

4. How can you *practically* apply the principles in this chapter to your life?

5

HELMET OF SALVATION

Ephesians 6:10–18;
Colossians 1:9–23

Having reviewed the first four pieces of armor, we now come to the *helmet of salvation*. As we cover this topic, it is my hope you have refreshed hope because you have the helmet of salvation. And if you do not have as your helmet or covering, Jesus, and all the hope He encapsulates, it is my desire you will! Romans 15:13 declares, *"Now* may the God of hope fill you with all joy and peace in believing, that you may abound in hope by the power of the Holy Spirit." This is my prayer for you, so let's not delay!

Christ: Our Covering, Our Source of Hope

As a blow to the head would be fatal for a soldier, soldiers in the apostle Paul's time wore helmets. Likewise, in illustrating our salvation as a helmet, Paul is letting us know the importance of not letting the enemy cause us to doubt that: Christ is *the* only hope for salvation and in Him our salvation is assured. First Thessalonians 5:8–9 states, "But let us, who are of the day, be sober putting on the breastplate of faith and love; and for an helmet, the hope of salvation. For God has not appointed us to wrath, but to obtain salvation by our Lord Jesus Christ." First Corinthians 1:18 declares, "For the message of the cross is foolishness to those who are perishing, but to us who are being saved it is the power of God." The enemy attempts to bring doubt, dread, fear, and discouragement into our hearts. It is all these things the helmet protects against. The helmet deals with our receiving Christ as Savior and the assurance of our eternal salvation as we *hold to our confession of faith*. It also represents the hope, peace, and encouragement that we received in Christ that we must not let the enemy steal. And we continue to grow in our salvation as we continually put on the helmet!

A closer look at our Salvation

Biblically speaking, salvation has happened to a believer, is happening, and will happen. The New Testament tells us we *have been saved* (Eph. 2:5), we *are being saved* (1 Cor. 1:18), and we *will be saved* (Matt. 10:22). Put another way, we can note that salvation covers three areas *justification*, *sanctification*, and *glorification*. Paul is speaking here to those already saved or *justified* by Christ. And they have and are being saved or sanctified in Christ, and the helmet is that they would remain confident in what they have received and in the full final work of Christ in them when they are glorified. Philippians 1:6 calls us to have faith that He (Chris)] who began a good work in us will see it to completion.

I think we have often neglected teaching these rich biblical terms in our churches, so let's look a little more at what is meant by these three areas.

Justification/Salvation: Simply, salvation means to be delivered or saved from something. In the New Testament (NT), it is used to refer to deliverance from the penalty/consequences of sin and into the kingdom of God. What is the penalty of sin, and how are we saved from it? Romans 6:23 states, "The wages of sin is death, but the gift of God is eternal life in Christ Jesus our Lord." The penalty is death or being eternally separated from God and in a place called hell. And everyone is born a sinner with this fate unless he or she receives the gift of salvation available to him or her in Christ. In speaking of this in John 3:16, Jesus said: "For God so loved the world, that he gave his only begotten Son, that whosoever believeth in Him should not perish, but have everlasting life." He goes on to clarify, though, that those who do not believe are condemned already and that the wrath of God abides on them (vv. 18, 36). Jesus did not have to come into the world to condemn it because it was condemned, so He came to offer the gift of salvation—to redeem!

We must know God abhors or hates sin, and as a perfect, holy, and righteous God, He had to punish it—because He is holy and righteous. Yet, because God also loves, He provided the most incredible substitute: Jesus. Our creator was willing out of love to take the penalty for our sin—to die in our place. On the cross, He became the Savior of all who would believe in Him for salvation. Salvation cannot be earned, only received (Eph. 2:8–9). So, it is in Christ alone that we are justified.

Sanctification: All throughout scripture the topic of sanctification is covered (Rom. 12; Eph.; James; John 17:17). In John 17:17 we read that Jesus prays that the Father would sanctify us in truth letting us know His word is truth. Being sanctified is what happened to us when we were saved and set apart for Christ. Sanctification is also what happens as we commit our ways to Him. We are sanctified in Christ and are being sanctified—just as we are saved and are being saved.

Glorification: We can have great hope and comfort by focusing on what Christ did on the cross then realizing after going through this to save us there is no way He will abandon us! With the helmet on, we can have the confidence Paul did in declaring "the sufferings of this present time are not worthy to be compared with the glory which shall be revealed in us" (Rom. 8:18).

Remain!

The truth is our faith is tested daily. In Luke 8 Jesus told a parable about a sower and the seed being the word of God/the gospel. And there were four varying results, and each of us will prove to be one. The first seed fell by the wayside, scripture says, and did not take root but was snatched away by the enemy, and they did not believe. The second seed fell on the stony ground, and the root did not go deep but quickly dried up. This group seemed to accept the message happily, but it did not last long. The stones represent temptation. The third seed fell on the thorny ground, and the thorns grew up with it and smothered it out. The thorns represent the cares, riches, and concerns of the world. *But* the fourth seed fell on the good soil, and it grew and produced a crop a hundredfold and remained. Don't give up! Don't give in to temptation! Don't let the things of the world get your focus off Christ. *Remain*! Remember what you were delivered from, and be fruitful—not in the power of your might but in the power of His might! Glory to God!

Be Encouraged

But we have an enemy that is going to try to get us to question our salvation or at the least bring discouragement into our lives. Second Corinthians 4:8–9, 14 declares, "We are troubled on every side, yet not distressed; we are perplexed, but not in despair; persecuted but not forsaken; cast down, but not destroyed. Knowing that he which raised up the Lord Jesus shall raise us up also with Jesus."

The helmet of salvation is the confidence that nothing will separate you from Christ. We can be fully confident of this because it is not us who did anything to save us, but as Ephesians 2 explains, Christ saved us by grace through faith, and our faith was even a gift according to Romans 12:3. It was all accomplished in what He did on the cross. Because of Christ, we who once were not a people, and at a time when we had no hope, Christ came and died for us, making an end to our sin and it consequences.

Knowing this should bring joy and peace to our lives. We also must guard against letting the enemy take the joy of our salvation. Many believers today need the joy of their salvation restored to them! Consider what you have in Christ. Don't let the enemy steal it. Put on the helmet of salvation!

We read in Colossians 1:9–23 that Paul desires for the church to be comforted or encouraged. Paul knew that when believers became discouraged, they weren't as enthusiastic about their faith. They would not have the zeal that keeps us growing in grace, and they also become easy prey for the world, the flesh, and the devil. So in Colossians, Paul reminds the church at Colossae of what they received in Christ and warns them against false teachings and deceit that only take away from what they received. As Paul states, he wants them strengthened according to His (Christ's) glorious power (v.

11). He wants them to have full assurance of how good and loving God is and in their salvation. Take time to read and consider who Colossians 1 tells us Christ is. How does this affect your faith?

Christianity is unique in that believers can have full assurance of their salvation through faith alone. It is not by having to do something— complete this task, be good enough, live a certain way, reach a certain level of spirituality. The assurance of the believer's salvation is in what Christ accomplished on the cross and faith in it alone!

Complete Assurance in Christ

Paul wanted us to understand that while we are in Christ, we are being conformed to His image, and we have the guarantee He will complete the work in us (Phil. 1:6) that He began. Being saved solely by what Christ did on the cross and nothing we did but to trust on what He did on the cross guarantees our position in Christ. This is a status to be enjoyed. We were made alive together with Christ (Eph. 2:1, 5). It is in the finished work of the cross that saves, not the cross plus!

Verse 15 of Colossians 2 declares on the cross Christ made a public spectacle of the enemy. As Leonard Ravenhill has explained, Christ's declaration on the cross that "It is finished" and then giving up His Spirit are the three greatest words ever uttered by the greatest man that ever lived![15] These three words will never be forgotten in heaven or hell or the implications reversed, as in saying these words Christ defeated the enemy, fulfilling God's plans for salvation once and for all on the cross. In declaring, "It is finished," Jesus declared all the Messianic prophecies fulfilled. The Old Testament law was fulfilled in its entirety, having remained faithful to the perfect will

---

[15] Leonard Ravenhill, "It is Finished." http://ravenhill.org/finished.htm

of the Father the power of sin was destroyed, and those who call on Christ and His work on the cross can have full assurance of their salvation. And rest knowing we have a sovereign God who, as King David proclaimed, has our times in His hands—no one else, not the enemy, no one! A lot of comfort can come into the life of one who truly gets this and holds onto it deep within him or herself!

Hebrews 10:22 says, "Let us draw near with a true heart in full assurance of faith, having our hearts sprinkled from an evil conscience, and our bodies washed with pure water." In Christ and Christ alone do we have the assurance of salvation and what assurance we DO have in Him!

Blessed Assurance
(Fanny Crosby c.1873)

Blessed assurance, Jesus is mine!
Oh, what a foretaste of glory divine!
Heir of salvation, purchase of God,
Born of His Spirit, washed in His blood.
This is my story; this is my song,
Praising my Savior all the day long;
This is my story; this is my song,
Praising my Savior all the day long.
Perfect submission, perfect delight,
Visions of rapture now burst on my sight;
Angels, descending, bring from above
Echoes of mercy, whispers of love.
Perfect submission, all is at rest,
I in my Savior am happy and blest[16]

---

[16] Fanny Crosby, "Blessed Assurance." c.1873. http://www.cyberhymnal. org/htm/b/l/e/blesseda.htm

Review/Application

1. Main Point(s): List what stood out to you:

2. What did you learn about:

   - yourself/human nature:

   - the enemy:

   - God:

3. What are the key scriptures that spoke to you and why?

4. How can you *practically* apply the principles in this chapter to your life?

6

ARMED WITH THE SWORD

Ephesians 6:17

"In the world, ye shall have tribulation: but be of good cheer; I have overcome the world." These words recorded of Jesus in John 16:33 declare that He has overcome the world. As previously covered, on the cross in proclaiming, "It is finished," He declared there is a rest for those who come to Him in faith, who trust in Him, and who live with His word being a lamp unto their feet and a light unto their path! You know, many people want to be free from things that concern or burden them but seem to be stuck, not able to get past issues or areas of trouble. The sword of the Spirit could just be the weapon they need to become skilled in using to overcome! We must remember that the wages of sin is death, but the gift of God is eternal life, abundant life in Christ (John 10:10). And Christ has given us a sword to help us obtain this life. Too many are not experiencing the freedom Christ died for them to have. Christ gave His life on a cross, not suffering for us just to continue to live the same as before. We talked about how John 8:31–32 proclaims if you abide in His word you are His disciples indeed and you shall know the truth, and the truth shall make you free. The words of John 8 are a promise and cover both the problem and the cure: before Christ, we are slaves to sin and sin's consequences and the word brings freedom. This word brings freedom by correcting wrong ways of believing and living. One way this word brings freedom is by using it as a sword.

Make Me Something New!

Too many people want to take Christ and add Him to the life they already have instead of living the life they can in Christ. Remember the lesson of the prodigal son who asked his father for his inheritance? He received his inheritance and then took it and wasted it with wayward living. But he found himself desperate—much worse off than before. He had to come to a place in his life where he understood it was more about coming to his father with an attitude of, "Make me (who you have created me to be)" rather than, "Give me." We too need a "make me" attitude rather than a "give me" attitude in our faith, and this is a big problem today. God has better plans for us than we can accomplish or become apart from Him. I love how in scripture when calling the disciples, Jesus tells them pretty much, "You will see this and experience this as My disciple." We see an excellent example of this in John 1:51, where Jesus tells Nathanael, "Verily, verily, I say unto you, Hereafter ye shall see the heaven open, and the angels of God ascending and descending upon the Son of Man." There was no way they could imagine the life Jesus had planned for them and what they would experience as His disciples. He had great plans to use them for His glory. They only needed to follow Him. We too only need to follow Him!

The enemy that we have does not want us to live in the victory

Christ won for us but instead comes to kill, steal, and destroy. As Christians, we are being assaulted by an enemy—and we are tempted to fall because of the tendencies of the flesh we still contend with. Scripture says the flesh wars against the spirit, so God gives us His armor so we can live by the Spirit. We must not forget that God knows what it takes to overcome the enemy. As Colossians 1 tells us, Christ created all things, and He is over every power or principality. So we are told to be strong in Him and the power of His might in Ephesians 6, relying entirely on Him.

Mighty in God!

In Judges 6–8 we read the story of Gideon. In Gideon, God gives an excellent example of how we can trust in Him to overcome for us. Being over the Israelite army, Gideon faced an enemy of approximately 135,000 troops. The Israelites were severely outnumbered, only having thirty-two thousand troops. Nonetheless, the Israelites led by Gideon readied themselves to do battle ... but God planned differently. God wanted to show His people just how powerful He was and how they could trust in Him. God instructed Gideon to let any of the soldiers who were fearful go. After this we read only ten thousand troops were left—twenty-two thousand went home. But God was not done yet. God then instructed Gideon to tell his troops to drink from the spring and those who drank from the water like a dog would stay to fight. After this, *only* three hundred remained! Think of the trust it would take for these three hundred to go against a hundred thirty-five thousand enemy troops. It calls us to question our faith.

We then read in Judges 7:20 that the army of the Israelites

surrounded the Midianites. On signal, they blew the trumpets and shouted, "The sword of the Lord and Gideon." And when they did, God brought chaos to the Midianites' camp, and they turned their swords against each other. So, in this God brought the Israelites a great victory! What a great lesson for us on how we can trust God. Remember, God even controls the chaos!

Of ourselves, we are weak to the schemes of the enemy. We are weak against the temptations of the flesh, but in God there is power! We have power for pulling down strongholds—power for walking in the victory Christ won for us! As 2 Corinthians 10:4 tells us, "The weapons of our warfare are not carnal, but mighty through God to the pulling down of strongholds."

Armed with Your Sword!

We have been talking about the armor God gives us to put on to stand against the schemes of the enemy. Here we come to the sixth piece of armor—the sword of the spirit—which is the word of God.

In Ephesians 6:17, we are called to take up the sword. Since we know the sword is the word of God, we know that if we don't know the word of God, we are not prepared or properly armed against the enemy. This is the problem we previously talked about as to why there's so much devastation in the church. Too many believers are going out into the battlefield and are not armed. We have to understand the importance of taking up the whole armor of God!

Believer, the call for you today is to be different than you were before Christ. And if you're going to be different than you were before Christ, you have to put on Christ, and in putting on Christ, we put on His armor!

When we receive Christ as our Savior, we receive the armor. We were given the armor; the call of the apostle Paul is for us to put it on! But if we're not going to put it on, if we're not going to know the word of God, the areas we are ignorant in are areas where we are not prepared and are vulnerable and defenseless to defend against. Satan does not want you to know the word of God because he wants you not to be prepared!

Prepare!

Author teacher John MacArthur tells us several ways that we prepare ourselves: (1) we read scripture; (2) we interpret what it means; (3) we correlate scriptures together, so we understand the whole counsel of God's word; and (4) we meditate on it and teach it.[17] And you know this teaching part is important. In working toward my masters of education degree, one thing that stood out to me as a Bible teacher was that teaching is really the capstone of learning. Maybe God knew what He was doing when He instructed us to be disciples, and then to disciple others. When we understand this, we understand discipleship is an important part of putting on the armor and not to be overlooked. As believers and churches, we must take discipleship as important as it is. It is a foundation of our faith! And it prepares us for the battle.

---

[17] John MacArthur, "The Armor of God: The Sword of the Spirit." Sermon Audio. 7/22/2012. http://www.sermonaudio.com/sermoninfo.asp?SID= 723121329493

Swords Are for Killing

Every other piece of armor is defensive. The sword is both defense and offensive. In using the sword, we are actively using the word of God against the schemes of the enemy (defensively). We also use the sword actively (or offensively) to crucify the flesh and its desires so we can live out our faith. This happens as we commit ourselves to learn the word and live the word. Hebrews 4:12 tells us the word of God is living and powerful and sharper than any two-edged sword. Paul only lists one offensive weapon because one weapon is all we need. That is the word of God! When combined with the Holy Spirit empowering you, the word is the power to change your life as well as overcoming the schemes of the enemy. Learn it and live it!

What it comes down to is actively pursuing God (to know Him and His ways) and to live godly. It is about loving God over loving the world. This is the lesson we learned about from 2 Timothy 3. At the beginning of this chapter, we read about those who call themselves believers but live to fulfill the desires of the flesh. They are lovers of pleasure and lovers of self over loving God. The last few verses of 2 Timothy 3 compare this to the true believer who uses the word to discipline him or herself toward godliness, as previously discussed. In doing this, they are offensively using the sword in their lives. First John 2 speaks to this as well. Verse 16 says all that is in the world, the lust of the flesh, and the lust of the eyes, are the pride of life and not from the Father but the world. We are to learn what is from God, and this is to be what we desire and practice. If we were to go to Matthew 4, we would see this is how Satan tempted Jesus, and Jesus responded by correcting Satan and going by God's will. Jesus used the word of God in each specific temptation offered to overcome the enemy. He humbled himself under God and resisted the enemy, and in doing so, we see the enemy flee!

How important is this word to you? Too many people are losing the battle because they're not using the sword. It is very sad, especially for those who have such access to the word of God. I spoke to someone recently who just returned from a missionary trip to Jamaica. He told me about a woman who was given the first Bible she ever owned. She just held it and cherished it, he said. It impacted him to see this and understand how we in America take the word for granted. Jesus treasured us and gave His life to redeem us. Do we treasure Him in return? Do we treasure the word of God? Do we realize what we have in the Bible and our great need for it in our lives? For this reason, many are not walking victoriously!

Review/Application

1. Main Point(s): List what stood out to you:

2. What did you learn about:

    - yourself/human nature:

    - the enemy:

    - God:

3. What are key scriptures that spoke to you and why?

4. How can you *practically* apply the principles in this chapter to your life?

7

GREAT IS THY FAITHFULNESS! PRAY, WATCH, PERSEVERE

Lamentations 3:19–25;
1 Samuel 23; Isaiah 30

As the time of His passion approached, we read in scripture that Jesus became *exceedingly* sorrowful and *deeply* distressed (Matt. 26:33–46). And we read that going off to pray, He *fell* to His face in prayer. In these descriptive words, we get a sense of how heavy His heart was and how great an event was about to take place. In considering Jesus was not only the Son of God but God Himself, how awesome the circumstances at hand must have been to trouble Him as such. Jesus was about to take the very wrath of God upon Himself—and for nothing He did. He was going to face the cross—the wrath of God in our place for our sin.

As a holy and righteous God, God had to judge sin when humankind sinned. Because of who He is, He could *not* ignore sin. And the wages of sin was death—eternal death. It was eternal punishment as there was no way humankind could ever settle the debt. Thankfully, even though He is righteous and holy and had to judge sin, He is equally loving and was willing to take the punishment of sin upon Himself. As the death of Christ was such a large sacrifice—being the Son of God—God has declared that any who call upon and trust what Jesus did on the cross in faith to cover *their* sin—having seen the need for a personal Savior—*would* be saved! How great a gift this is! We deserved death, but God, knowing we could not save ourselves, out of His love, grace, and mercy provided a way—the only way (John 14:6) in Christ.

Consider the wrath of God. God is perfect and does everything to perfection—even His wrath. The events Jesus knew were about to take place deeply troubled Him. Wasn't there another way? How could God allow His Son to face the cross and take on the very wrath of God for our sin? Truly the answer is *no*. There was no other way; otherwise Christ would not have faced the cross. God would have provided the other way. A loving God would have spared His Son if there was another way to pardon our sin, but there wasn't, so because of His love for us, He allowed His Son to face the cross.

As He prepared for this great trial, Jesus fell to His knees in prayer. To prepare for the great battle He faced—He prayed. This should be a great example for us. I think we often fail because we have not first prepared for the battle. Often when we go through studies on the armor of God, prayer is not included as a piece of armor. It is often thrown in as kind of a side issue, thrown in as something else we do along with putting on the armor. But often prayer is presented in a way that does not give it the full attention I think it needs and the full force of weight it brings to our success as we walk in our faith. I believe prayer can be counted as another piece of armor. Prayer was important to Jesus as He faced His greatest challenge and is equally critical to our success. In fact, if the apostle Paul took the time to tell us to take everything to God in prayer (Eph. 6:18), it must have been because he knew we could expect results. He knew prayer was a powerful weapon!

Right Prayers—Bold Prayers!

Reading through the New Testament, we could note several things that can hinder our prayers. These include: not asking, selfishness (in requests/giving) (James 4:3–4), doubt/lack of faith (Mark 11:22–29), sin/disobedience (including unforgiveness) (Ps. 66:18; Isa. 59:1-2,) idolatry (Jer. 11:10–14), neglecting the needy (Prov. 21:13), and relationships (spousal/un-reconciliation in general) (1 Peter 3:7). Yet, where I started this list is probably the saddest reason—having no results from a prayer life simply because we don't pray! As for the other reasons, they are important, and we do need to address them. I think as we devote ourselves to the word of God and honoring God with our lives, we will naturally want to work on each. And if we are involved with God, we definitely will be seeking Him in prayer!

Consider Psalm 37:4, where we read God will "give us the desires of our heart." What a great promise, and we have often heard this quoted. But if we look at the first part of this scripture that says, "Take delight in the Lord," we get some great insight. If we are taking delight in the Lord, we are seeking Him and learning about Him through His word. We are learning how He thinks and what He desires, and what results is that we will delight in the things He delights! As we delight in the Lord what we desire will change to the things He desires!

It amazes me to think that a Christian would have a need and not go to God about it. And if we examined ourselves, we would see we are all guilty of this to some degree. James 4:2–3 tells us we "have not because we ask not." And it goes on to say we ask and do not have because we "ask amiss." We ask for things selfishly that are truly outside the will of God and that in His divine knowledge He does not give us because it is not truly good for us. If it were, He would give it to us. He gives every good thing to His people. Nonetheless, God wants us to be bold in our prayers. He wants us to come boldly to the throne of grace and mercy and as Paul stated in Ephesians 6:18, to take everything to God in prayer. Just pray! Don't neglect this wonderful opportunity to take everything to God!

You know it truly is a shame that people do not take time to go before the throne of God as often as they could. Consider some of the areas we may lack in only because we do not ask—not just tangible items but even joy, peace, and happiness. We do not ask God or inquire of Him for decisions in our lives and find ourselves making decisions or doing things outside His will for us and pay the consequences. We are called to go boldly before the throne of grace and mercy to find help in our time of need. I think our ministry and our churches could benefit greatly by taking this to heart. While our prayers should not be selfish, they should be bold! Are your prayers bold? Are your prayer requests things that take a mighty movement of God to happen? Let's pray boldly!

In Ephesians 6:18 Paul wanted us to "pray always with all prayer and supplication in the Spirit, and watching thereunto with all perseverance and supplication for all the saints." He instructed us to pray for our walk and needs and the church/other believers. This is a recipe for revival! As believers look to and show their dependence on God, He will show Himself strong on their behalf. Putting on the armor of God is about seeking after God and relying on Him and His power constantly, and we know "Without faith it is impossible to please God" and God is a "rewarder of those that diligently seek Him" (Heb. 11:6). Now let's look at an example in King David of how we are to approach and rely on God and the results.

Two Approaches

In 1 Samuel 23, we find the narrative of David being pursued by Saul and his army. Word came to David that the Philistines were invading the town of Keilah (kay-ee-la). Despite the pressure he was under, he took time and called the priest and inquired of the Lord to decide if he should go down to Keilah to help against the Philistines. The answer was to go and that God would give Him the victory. The point is that David took time to inquire of the Lord before making such a big decision and then believed the word of the Lord. (As a side note, you know the word of God has so many promises just waiting for believers to believe in them for themselves!) Now David could have easily said, "I am too busy for this," but here he showed wisdom in seeking what the Lord would have him do. How many times do we not take time to inquire of the Lord because we're too busy? David was successful here because he took the time to inquire of the Lord. Now, of course, this was under the old covenant in that we see David call the priest and later kings would inquire through prophets or seers, but we under the new covenant are to go directly to God in prayer. We don't go to priest or prophets! In fact, under the new covenant, believers in general are referred to as a royal priesthood. I want you to get this. While David was anointed and used mightily in the salvation plan, and he was royalty on earth, he had to go to the priest to inquire of God. But we can go directly to the throne and inquire for ourselves with Jesus as our High Priest. What an opportunity!

Now let's shift our attention to Saul in 1 Samuel 23 in contrast to David and how he often conducted his life. Saul often directed his *own* decisions/steps going along, making all the decisions for himself when there were times when he should have sought the Lord or followed God's word. Whatever felt right to Saul was what Saul often did. And if something good happened—or if he thought so—as in when he heard of David being in Keilah (1 Sam. 23:7) and thought he had him trapped, he credited God for his good fortune. In verse 7 we read Saul declared, "God hath delivered him into my hand; for he is shut in, by entering into a town that hath gates and bars." "Well praise God," Saul declared and thought God was working on his behalf where if we would read this narrative we find Saul never even sought God in this situation. In fact, Saul not only never inquired of God in these passages but he was working against the plans of God. I wonder in our own lives how many times we struggle because we are going against God's plans for us.

Additionally, while at times we neglect seeing if God has something to say about a situation, too often we go to another source for help while ignoring what God says. In Isaiah 30:1-7 we see Judah going to Egypt to ask for help. And God warns them of the correction that comes with relying on another but not Him, yet He also promises them grace. God promises that He will reveal Himself to His people. He will continue to prophesy to His people to bring teaching and correction to them. He offers grace. The question for us is, where do we go for help? Do we include God in our decisions and if He has anything to say about what we are facing in His word?

We in many ways are not much different than Saul or these Israelites. We many times seek counsel of the world yet do not inquire of God or wait on Him. Yet we do not want to hear about the correction of God or reap what we sow from bad decisions, or that our struggles may very well be because we have set ourselves up in opposition to the plans of God and make no mistake His plans will prevail. But we just want to hear about grace. We, like the Israelites, don't want correction or conviction.

To seek after and follow God means our lives are going to require change. What we desire should begin to align with what God desires, what He wills. We must be like David in knowing what God desires and take bold action!

First Chronicles 10:13 states, "So Saul died for his unfaithfulness which he had committed against the Lord, because he did not keep the word of the Lord, and also because he consulted with a medium for guidance." In this we see that Saul lost the kingdom and ultimately his life by not keeping the commands of the Lord, seeking guidance elsewhere, and not inquiring of the Lord. And there are other examples throughout scripture of those who suffered because they just did their own thing and those who triumphed and were saved because they took the time to inquire of the Lord. King Jehoshaphat is another good example of one who triumphed against great odds because he took time to inquire of the Lord and put his faith not in his ability but in God's ability and God, trusting God to be faithful to His word (2 Chronicles 20). Go to God and trust Him!

What a Friend We Have

Life can be busy, but we must not neglect to take the time to inquire of the Lord in making decisions in our lives, churches, community, and even country; if so, we must be prepared to reap what we sow. We have too often neglected to recognize God's hand in all things, praised Him often, thanked Him, and gone to Him as we could have and suffered as a result. As the great old hymn says, "What a friend we have in Jesus all our sins and griefs to bear. O what help we often forfeit, O what needless pain we bear. All because we do not carry everything to God in prayer."[18] In Hebrews 4:16 we are encouraged to come boldly before the throne of grace, that we may obtain mercy and find grace to help in our time of need. Or as Paul tells us in Ephesians 6, "Pray always!" We likely all have needs in areas we could benefit greatly by seeking God's help.

Random House dictionary defines inquire as "to seek information by asking[19]." Therefore, when we inquire of God, we seek His will or desire in a situation. We need to take time to pray and seek God in all things. When we inquire of the Lord, it demonstrates our trust in Him. It shows we have faith that God knows best and we want what He desires. We may ask for something specific but trust the actual results to Him. Consider Jesus's prayer in the garden from our opening. Jesus was in great distress, and He prayed, "If possible lift this cup from me. Nevertheless not my will, but your will be done (Luke 22:42)." No matter what, He trusted God … His faith was not based on the answer or situation. He trusted the sovereign God period!

When we inquire of the Lord, it shows our confidence in Him. It demonstrates that we have faith that God knows what is best for

---

[18] Joseph M. Scriven, "What A Friend We Have in Jesus." c. 1855. http://www.cyberhymnal.org/htm/w/a/f/wafwhij.htm

[19] inquire. Dictionary.com. *Dictionary.com Unabridged*. Random House, Inc. http://www.dictionary.com/browse/inquire(accessed: August 8, 2017).

us and we want what He desires. If we are not inquiring of the Lord, we are going off of our own desires or the counsel of the enemy (Isa. 30:1–3). Who we go to truly reflects who we put our trust in. Too often I am afraid we put our trust in our own wisdom and abilities. What truly made David the man he was (and we understand that he too failed from time to time) was that he inquired of the Lord, put his faith in God's ability, not his own, and was willing to repent and turn to God in areas where he did falter. In his heart he truly wanted what God wanted, even though he sometimes missed the mark.

The Spirit Is Willing!

Fortunately, when we are unfaithful, God's faithfulness continually prompts us to pray, to seek Him, and to inquire of Him. His faithfulness exceeds our sin. His faithfulness exceeds our unfaithfulness. When I consider this, I must exclaim with the prophet Jeremiah who mourned for God's people, "Truly great is Thy faithfulness!"

In going to the cross, Jesus could boldly do it because He knew the heavenly Father could be trusted. And in considering prayer, He told His disciples to "watch and pray, lest you enter into temptation. The Spirit indeed is willing, but the flesh is weak" (Matt. 26:41). What importance this message puts on our prayer life to win the battle. I am convinced our walk of faith, our ministry, what we have in Christ will never exceed our prayer life! What a great encouragement for us as the apostle Paul similarly tells us in Ephesians 6:18 to "pray always with all prayer and supplication in the Spirit, being watchful to this end with all perseverance and supplication for all the saints." Pray not just for ourselves but all the saints. Let's not underestimate the power of prayer! In fact, the prayer of a believer directed at such an awesome mighty God—even if the faith behind it only amounts to faith the size of a mustard seed—can move mountains! What a mighty God we serve!

Be watchful, always pray, and persevere!

Review/Application

1. Main Point(s): List what stood out to you:

2. What did you learn about:

    - yourself/human nature:

    - the enemy:

    - God:

3. What are key scriptures that spoke to you and why?

4. How can you *practically* apply the principles in this chapter to your life?

8

TASTE AND SEE THAT
THE LORD IS GOOD!

In his book *The Wonders of the Word of God*, Evangelist Robert L. Sumner tells about a man in Kansas City who was severely injured in an explosion.[20] The victim's face was badly disfigured, and he lost his eyesight as well as both hands. As just a new Christian, one of his greatest disappointments was that he could no longer read the Bible. Then he heard about a lady in England who read Braille with her lips. Hoping to do the same, he sent for some books of the Bible in Braille. Much to his dismay, however, he discovered that the nerve endings in his lips had been destroyed by the explosion. One day, as he brought one of the Braille pages to his lips, his tongue happened to touch a few of the raised characters, and he could feel them. Like a flash he thought, *I can read the Bible using my tongue*. At the time

---

[20] Robert L. Sumner, *The Wonders of the Word of God*. (Lynchburg, VA: Biblical Evangelism Press, 1969).

Robert Sumner wrote his book in 1969, the man had "read" through the entire Bible four times.

Talk about tasting how good the Lord is (Ps. 34:8)! In reading this story, I can't help but consider the revival there would be if many more Christians desired the word of God as such! The word of God was obviously vital to this man. It was likely a great source of hope to him during this hard time in life. I ask, where do you draw your hope? How important is this word to you? Have you ever gone through a time, maybe like this man, where you hungered for the word of God? If so you will have realized what Matthew 5 declared in saying those that hunger and thirst for righteousness shall be filled. God is all that is going to fill the hunger/what's lacking in a believer's life. How important is this word to you? The Bible is so important to believers! While it is what Jesus says brings freedom (John 8:31–32), it is too often neglected, and then freedom is lost to bondage. How important is the word to you and your life? The truth is many of us probably have multiple Bibles in our homes in America but don't open them and wonder why we have the troubles we do! Some believers/churches in the world are lucky to have one. What they must think of us who take it for granted! The importance of the Word was displayed in the apostle Paul, who asked for the word in his final days. The comfort it must have brought to him in that dark, dreary holding cell.

I ask again, how important is the word of God to you? Is it what brings you hope and comfort in life? Is it important to you as you desire to know more about your Savior and who you were created to be in Him?

Jesus expected His disciples to abide in His word. As Jesus declares to us in John 8:31–32, it is *abiding* in His word that brings freedom in our lives. The word of God activated in the lives of

Spirit-filled, born-again believers is powerful! It is the power of God to change lives! This is why the enemy would want us to be distracted or too busy for the word and neglect it. And so, let's look at how it affects the lives of believers as they engage in it. We should desire the word of God in our lives because we know it to be a gift from God. It is a means of grace that is not only good for us but necessary for us if we are to live the life Christ died for us to have.

Living the Life Christ Died for You to Have

Second Timothy 3:16 declares that we need this word for "correction, for instruction in righteousness, that the man of God may be complete, thoroughly equipped for every good work." And it is these items we are going to look into further. we know if this word corrects us and equips us to live the plans God has for us, we can be sure the converse is true—without it, we will not be equipped or be prepared to walk in the way Christ would have us!

We need the Word to transform us as 2 Timothy 3 declares. Pastor David Guzik states of these verses: "When we come to the Bible and let God speak to us, it changes us—it makes us complete and transforms us." He states:

> One way the Bible transforms us is through our understanding. Romans 12:2 says, do not be conformed to this world, but be transformed by the renewing of your mind, that you may prove what is that good and acceptable and perfect will of God. When we let the Bible guide our thinking, our minds are renewed and transformed, so we begin actually to think as God thinks (we previously reviewed Romans 12 and it's recipe for change).

But there is another level by which the Bible transforms us: by a spiritual work, a spiritual blessing which God works in us as we come to the Bible and let Him speak to us. This is a spiritual work that goes beyond our intellectual understanding. With great spiritual power beyond our intellect:

- The Bible gives us eternal life (1 Peter 1:23).
- The Bible spiritually cleanses us (Ephesians 5:26).
- The Bible gives us power against demonic spirits (Ephesians 6:17).
- The Bible brings spiritual power to heal our bodies (Matthew 8:16).
- The Bible brings us spiritual strength (Psalm 119:28).
- The Bible has the power to spiritually build faith in us (Romans 10:17). [21]

God gave us His word to guide us. It is to be a lamp unto our feet and a light unto our path. It is to teach us how to live life; what choices to make; what conversation is and isn't appropriate; what attitudes to take on; what is sin; what is holy; how to be a spouse; how to be a parent; how to be a child; how to be a friend; how to edify, encourage, and correct others; how to react to life's problems; and how to have empathy and compassion toward others. It is the empowerment to do something about it and how to love God and love others. We are saved solely by grace and what Christ accomplished on the cross. It is through the word that we are encouraged to persevere—to remain.

---

[21] D. Guzik, "Study Guide for 2 Timothy 3 by David Guzik." *Blue Letter Bible*. Last Modified 7 Jul, 2006. https://www.blueletterbible.org/Comm/guzik_david/StudyGuide_2Ti/2Ti_3.cfm

Take Heart!

We would be ignoring an obvious truth and deceive ourselves to attempt to believe that the world we live in is all rosy and flowery and that once we become Christians that we will no longer face trouble. The reality is we all will face difficulties in life. But in Christ, as we put on the character of Christ, we learn how to have still a peace that surpasses all understanding. In Christ, we can do as declared in the book of James and count it all joy when faced with various trials because we know they are building Christlike character in us as we follow His guidance.

As already mentioned, the word encourages us, and God uses it to sustain us through all life's challenges it prepares us to stand against temptation. In John 16:33 we read the words of Jesus as He states, "These things I have spoken to you, that in me you may have peace. In the world you will have tribulation: but be of good cheer; I have overcome the world." A couple of things to note. He says in Him we might have peace. He uses might as we have the responsibility to let nothing steal this peace from us! No matter what you face, do not let it steal what you have in Christ, for even though we know we shall have tribulation, we know Christ has overcome!

I would like to share a personal story of hope and God's sustaining power. My wife and I are not immune to life's struggles. We have had many struggles throughout our lives. The truth is that my wife struggles every day. Years ago, we received a great blessing from God when our twins were born, but my wife also developed at this time what they labeled fibromyalgia. She desired her whole life to have kids and always talked about how she would love to have twins. After having two previous children, she was pregnant again and this time with twins! It was an exciting time. However, due to the strain on her body, she found herself struggling with unbearable pain coupled with bouts of depression as a result. The pain was so that she could not even play and dance with her new babies if she wanted. It was hard for her, but she knew because of the word of God, she had hope! She clung to Romans 8:28, which declares, "God works all things for the good of those who love Him who are called according to His purpose."

My wife has mostly been delivered from that crippling pain. Never lose hope! Hope hopes against all hope. The world told my wife she would not get better and that she would always struggle. God said differently!

In Romans 4 we read the account of Abraham, who became a father to Isaac at the age of one hundred. When Abraham was one hundred, his wife Sarah was ninety. At this age, one would usually believe that Sarah was much beyond her childbearing years. However, of Abraham, we read that, "Against all hope, Abraham in hope believed" (Rom. 4:18). Abraham chose to believe the word of God over anything else. As Jesus is the same yesterday, today, and forever, we too are invited to always hope against all hope!

You Can't Gain What You Need from the Word without Being in the Word!

In John 10:10 Jesus is quoted as saying, "The thief cometh not, but for to steal, and to kill, and to destroy. I come that they might have life and that they might have it more abundantly." In Deuteronomy 30:19 God told His people, "I have set before you life and death, blessing and cursing: therefore choose life." These verses give us great direction. While this word gives life to those who believe on it and then continues to free those that continue in it, the enemy likewise has plans for you. We must be alert to this fact and be in the Word! Notice the use of the words *might* from John 10 (similar to what we discussed of John 8) and *choose* from Deuteronomy 30. We have to agree with God and then commit our ways to Him to have and be all He desires for us!

Consider what God told Joshua in Joshua 1:7–9. It states:

> Only be strong and *very* courageous, that you may observe to do according to *all* the law which Moses my servant commanded you; do *not* turn from it to the right hand or to the left, that you may prosper wherever you go. This book of the law shall *not* depart from your mouth, but you shall meditate in it day and night, that you may observe to do according to *all* that is written in it. For *then* you *will* make your way prosperous, and then you will have good success.

I accentuated several words here for emphasis. Note God's instructions to Joshua on how important heeding the words of God was to Joshua's success. Joshua's success was going to come from His relationship with God and believing in the promises of God. Joshua had to look to and trust God. The word *meditate* used here is more than *think*ing on but also includes to act on. Joshua did not know what lie ahead, but with God giving him the direction and Joshua following after Him, God would also give the victory. These words to should encourage us. We can be victorious as Joshua was. The promise here was from Moses to Joshua down to us!

I would like to challenge everyone to regular scripture intake. Get a Bible-reading plan and go with it, and if you do miss a day or two, just like exercising, just start back up and come back later to get the days you missed if need be. There are many different plans to get you through the Bible. Many people's Bibles have a plan in them. Personally, I like to just alternate between reading an Old and New Testament book and then highlighting in front of my Bible when I complete a book. This lets me track my progress. Whatever works for you—find a plan that you think will work for you and start! And if/when you miss a day or so, start in again. Just do it!

Besides reading, there are many ways for us to get the word in us (i.e., sermons, teachings, recordings). But we must get it in us. Nothing replaces reading the word for ourselves and meditating on it, but for some, this is not possible. Some in nursing homes may need others to read to them. Some may not know how to read. But we must desire the word. We must make it a part of our lives.

Results of Going It on Our Own

While we used the great example of Joshua, we also note he was not perfect. One time he did not confer with God and made a peace treaty with those from Gideon (Joshua 9). Joshua used his own judgement, and what would eventually come from this is the ways of the enemy influencing God's people. God's instruction to the Israelites to purge the land of all foreigners and foreign ways still apply today. We are to repent or turn our way of thinking to align with God and way of being to His ways. In short, when we come to Christ and as we nurture our relationship with Him and walk in His truth, we are changed from the inside out.

I am afraid we have made peace with the world, at times forsaking of the truth! Joshua going against God's word allowed a way in for the enemy. Experience *is not* always the best answer. We can learn from God and save a lot of trouble! The only experience that is best to learn from is experiencing freedom from trusting God!

So we can be successful in learning and living as Christians, Christ told us that He was sending us a helper—the Holy Spirit—who would lead us into all truth and teach us all truth. Christ says in John 14:6 He is the only truth. Likewise, Christ prayed in John 17:17 that the Father would sanctify believers in truth and that His word is truth. The Holy Spirit is in believers and those who yield to Him, who deny themselves daily and carry their cross, are changed from glory to glory. The word of God is living and powerful and has the ability to do this for those who get the word in them. And *nothing* can replace it in our lives!

We go along on our own so often as if we can do it on our own. We *can't* do it on our own. Hosea 4:6 declares, "My people are destroyed for lack of knowledge." Lack of knowledge is one of the greatest problems in the church today, and there is only one way to get past this problem—the Word! This word, as Romans 12 tells us, is given to transform our way of thinking. In 2 Corinthians 10:3–6, we are taught that when we come to Christ, we have these strongholds built up in us. This word is the only thing that tears them down and makes Christ our stronghold.

Growing in Faith

Several years ago while flipping the channels, I saw a popular talk show was having spirituality week. Knowing many people are facing challenging times and looking for hope, and thinking there must be more in life at times, this talk show host decided to try and help people understand what spirituality truly is and find peace. She had on her show what she claimed to be some of the world's "leading spiritual teachers." And she was right in the fact at least that they were of the world. Worldly in their views and opinions is all they were. None of them once covered the truths of sin and the need to be saved. None of them pointed to Christ as the only truth—the only way!

The focus of these spiritual "experts" was for people to look at self. Oh, how I dread the fate of such a belief, such a world. There was a brave lady in the audience who did stand up and announce Jesus as the only name under heaven that one can be saved. Was she dismissed? Yes, mainly. But she showed the example for us. If the church of Christ is not going to lift up Christ in their lives, no one else will! There are a lot of untruths out there. We have a privilege of pointing others to the one true God—Jesus. *The world focuses on the wrong things for hope. We must not do the same!*

We must focus on Christ and grow in our relationship with Him. It is in this that we have success. Scripture tells us faith comes by hearing and hearing by the word of God (Rom. 10:17). It is in Christ that we understand our identity, and we must accept who and what God says we are, and we learn about this identity in the word.

The Truth *Shall* Make You Free!

Perhaps you are reading this and have never put your trust in Christ, never receiving Him as your Savior. You want to receive the freedom Jesus told about in John 8:31–32 in stating, "If you continue in my word, you are my disciple indeed, and you shall know the truth and the truth shall make you free." If you know you have things in life keeping you prisoner, Jesus promise to enter your life through the Holy Spirit and never to leave you nor forsake you. He promises to stay with you, guide you, and help you through ... just as He was with Joshua. He tells you that if you learn from Him, you will find rest for your soul (Matt. 11:28–30). Just by calling on the name of the Jesus, admitting you're a sinner needing a Savior, and then claiming the gift of salvation available through Christ, you can be saved!

Christ loved you so much and knew that you could not save yourself, so He came and offered His own life as a sacrifice. And God the Father has acknowledged the death of His Son was such a huge sacrifice and declared it is enough to save anyone who calls on His name. In doing this, God accounts His sacrifice to you, covering your sin. God no longer sees you in your sin state when you trust in Jesus for salvation. God looks at you and sees Christ and His holiness! While the Bible says death was the judgment for sin and there is an eternal place of torment for those who do not repent and believe on Christ, this does not have to be your fate. You can trust on the Lord Jesus today! What a great gift!

It is God's holy word that reveals this gospel to us and the Holy Spirit that causes us to be able to see this truth. It all points to Jesus. Do you know Him today? And if you do, don't you want to know Him better?

Review/Application

1. Main Point(s): List what stood out to you:

2. What did you learn about:

    - yourself/human nature:

    - the enemy:

    - God:

3. What are key scriptures that spoke to you and why?

4. How can you *practically* apply the principles in this chapter to your life?

9

LET *GOD* BE TRUE AND EVERY MAN A LIAR

There are three questions that many people have been wondering for hundreds, if not thousands of years: can the Bible be trusted, what makes the Bible different from than any other religious text, and how is Christianity any different from other religions? We are going to look at the topic in theology known as apologetics. Apologetics is defined as a branch of theology devoted to the defense of the divine origin and authority of Christianity. In other words, we are going to examine why we can believe what we believe and why we can rely on the Bible.

We need to hold, or esteem, the Bible correctly in order to get the most from it. Why? Because if the authority and truth of the Bible is lowered even slightly in our minds then we will not take the Bible seriously, and therefore its effect on our lives will be diminished. We *must not* take it for granted or forget that this is the *word of God!* When people get this reality in them, they start to view the word in a different light. It suddenly becomes more important to them.

Previously, we talked about how spiritual disciplines are gifts which help us to grow in God's grace. Studying the Bible is probably the most important of the spiritual disciplines. However, the practice of reading and studying scripture has taken a back seat in the lives of many. In fact, most people have never read the Bible. Sadly, many Christians never even read the Bible. According to a study by Barna Research Group, only about 14 percent of Americans claim to read their Bible daily. While a majority of Bible readers (52 percent) claim to read it only three to four times per year.[22] I would note that while even a small amount is better than nothing, there is a difference between a casual reading of the word and studying it.

Take a moment to imagine that the very thing that Jesus says will bring us freedom, many ignore. While there are likely multiple reasons for this, the primary reason is nothing more than neglect. Whatever the reason, we are going to look at the Bible afresh and how to put its power to work in our lives.

First, we need to know that we can believe the Bible and all of its truths. As believers, we must go to and rely on the word over and above any other source, acknowledging that there is nothing greater on which we can rely! To go to some other source first would be to imply that it is a higher authority. In dealing with the question, "Can the Bible be trusted?" The answer is simple. The Bible testifies of itself that it is the truth, and as such we can have confidence in all that it says! In considering a defense of the word, I thought about Charles Spurgeon saying, "The Word of God is like a lion. You don't have to defend a lion. All you have to do is let the

---

[22] Barna Group. State of the Bible 2015. http://www.americanbible.org/uploads/content/State_of_the_Bible_2015_report.pdf

lion loose and the lion will defend itself!"[23] Now this is not to say Spurgeon meant we do not defend the truths of scripture. Rather it is likely Spurgeon was referencing the effectiveness of proclaiming God's word. Or to those whom the Holy Spirit opens the eyes of their hearts, they need no convincing. The Holy Spirit testifies to their spirits that the word is truth. Even so, we know the Bible can be relied upon.

The world would have you to believe that the Bible is only partly true. We need to know that the Bible is everything that it claims to be; believing anything else would be allowing the enemy to steal the power which is available in God's word. A proper view of the Bible is to esteem God's word while having a reverence for it. When we do this, the Bible will have its rightful place in our lives as Christians and the word will bring forth change into our lives.

Some might use man's knowledge (which is foolishness to God) to say, "Well, what about the evidence or issues that should cause one to doubt the authenticity of the Bible?" Let's examine a few of these areas. Albeit each topic could be a chapter or even book all its own, I think in even a brief review we can see how many have believed a lie.

Reliability

Can the Bible be relied upon? After all, it was written by man. The Bible is unique in that it is not just a written work by one person, but rather a collection of writings or historical documents. These writings were written by over forty authors which spanned over

---

[23] David Kowalski, "Charles Spurgeon on Defending the faith." ApologeticsIndex. April 30, 2013. http://www.apologeticsindex.org/3030-spurgeon-defending-the-faith

three different continents and spoken in three languages (Hebrew, Greek, Aramaic). Although it was written over a period of fifteen hundred years, each book fit together perfectly while collaborate and supporting one other. Amazingly, all of these books point to one primary source: Christ! This is not just one document making a claim; many of the writings were done by actual eyewitnesses to each event in the presence of other eyewitnesses. This means that someone could have spoken out if they saw something other than what was being written. Scholars admit that this collection of books is a historically reliable and credible document.

Well, how about how much it has been *translated*? Doesn't that make it questionable? As teacher Voddie Bauchman explains that truth, if one understood this, it is laughable to think the translations are not reliable.[24] We already covered many of the reasons for this, but on top of this, we have over six thousand historical texts for the New Testament dating back to the beginning of the second century, and they all corroborate each other—even those from various continents in different languages. This is pretty remarkable!

Other Evidence Against (Archaeology, Science)

In regard to any archaeological findings and the Bible, Dr. Nelson Glueck, probably the greatest modern authority on Israeli archaeology, reminds us, "*No* archaeological discovery has ever controverted a biblical reference. Scores of archaeological findings have confirmed in clear outline or exact detail historical statements in the Bible. And, by the same token, proper evaluation of Biblical descriptions

---

[24] Voddie Bauchman, "Why I Choose to Believe the Bible." Sermon Audio. 6/30/2005. http://www.sermonaudio.com/sermoninfo.asp?SID=530914253

has often led to amazing discoveries."[25] Simply, no archaeological findings have ever disproved but only at the end of the day supported biblical narratives.

But the Science!

Okay, how about all the scientific "facts" against scripture? We could spend a whole day on this one question. Truth—none of them disprove the Bible. For instance, the one that comes to my mind is of the earth being round. Long before modern science thought it, Isaiah 40:22 told us the earth is round. And there are many other such examples from the Bible. If we Christians understood the word of God as we should, we might live in a different world.

The enemy is going to do what he has always done—try to tear down the Bible. Consider that just a hundred years ago in our schools, creationism was the common teaching in America. This has reversed now, where evolution is the norm and creationism is not allowed. And honestly, the theory of evolution could more easily be argued not to be intelligible. What we now know of a cell (through modern microscopes) we know that if any part is not there or functioning, a cell is dead. It cannot evolve.

When you get in the word of God and start to realize that hundreds of prophecies were made by God's prophets that later came to be hundreds of years later and that the Bible had over forty authors whose works support each other, you will start to see it as the

---

[25] Dr. Nelson Glueck "Sunday Quote: Nelson Glueck on Archaeology." Apologetics 315. http://www.apologetics315.com/2009/07/sunday-quote-nelson-glueck-on.html

miraculous work it is! Indeed, considering all this, let God be true and every man a liar (Rom. 3:4)!

We must not let the world influence us differently on the reliability of the Bible and in doing so weaken our faith! As noted in John 1, Jesus is the word made flesh. In John 14:6 Jesus says He is the truth and goes on to say in verses 16–17 that the Spirit of truth lives in believers and the world cannot receive this truth because it does not know Christ. We need to go with the word because it is truth.

Why can't the world just acknowledge the Bible as truth? Because then it has to deal with the implications. And knowing the word is truth, we believers also have to deal with the implications of it!

The Necessity of the Word

John 1 also states that in the beginning was the word and the word was with God, and the Word was God. John 1 goes on to say the word became flesh and dwelt among us. Know that this word is the word of God, and after having ascertained it can be relied on and that this word became flesh through Jesus. We need to have this revelation of how great this word is and as such how powerful it can be in our lives. In fact, in John 1 it says in Him—the Word that became flesh—was life. Let's review a few of the truths we have covered that demonstrates its necessity in the life of a believer.

In John 8:31–32 we read, "Then Jesus said to those Jews who believed Him, 'If you abide in My word, you are My disciples indeed, and you shall know the truth, and the truth shall make you free." Many people want to live a victorious life. The truth is the word of God equips believers to live victoriously (Eph. 6/full armor). Jesus in this scripture was speaking to believers, so we know first to be empowered one has to believe in Him.

First Peter 1:23 declares that as believers we were not born of corruptible seed but incorruptible, through the word of God which lives and abides forever. This word is not corrupted by man or this world, as many would believe, but God has inspired this word, and as this verse declares, it is not corrupt. God has preserved the overall truths of scripture. As covered previously, 2 Timothy 3:16 says, "All scripture is inspired of God. And is profitable for reproof, for *training* in righteousness, that the man of God may be thoroughly complete … lacking nothing!" Note it is profitable for training. *Obedience is trained!*

First Peter 1:25 and 2:2 say, "But the word of the Lord endureth forever. And this is the word which by the gospel is preached to you. As newborn babes, desire the pure milk of the word, that you may grow thereby." We need this word to grow. We need to have regular nourishment. In the flesh, if we do not get regular nourishment, we die. It is the same spiritually this word is the bread of life, given to nourish us!

I hear people saying to themselves, "Well I just don't read" or "I don't enjoy reading." You may want to start! Jesus said that man shall not live by bread alone but by every word. Jesus's thought here was that believers would read the entire Bible. Why? Because it's good for you, and because it pleases God, because it is the sword of the spirit that conquers the enemy! Because it is God's word and God's word has immeasurable value and we should desire it! When we get a real revelation of what this book is, we truly know our great need for it and truly know what a wonderful gift it is, one not to be taken for granted!

When Christ walked the earth, we see the world rejected Him

and ultimately crucified Him (John 18:37–40). The world still stands in rejection. Let us not dare do the same today, Instead, let us reject the world and put our faith wholeheartedly in Christ and embrace the gift of His word He has given us!

> *We must not only be armed with truth; we also*
> *must actively put it into practice in our life!*

Review/Application

1. Main Point(s): List what stood out to you:

2. What did you learn about:

     - yourself/human nature:

     - the enemy:

     - God:

3. What are key scriptures that spoke to you and why?

4. How can you *practically* apply the principles in this chapter to your life?

10

FREE AT *LAST!*

In Ephesians 6 the apostle Paul reminds us that we are in a war. A battle pursues, and what is at stake is believers living free from sin and bondage and for the gospel message to continue going forth. And in understanding this, 1 Peter 5:8 calls believers to "be sober, be vigilant," understanding there *is* an enemy roaming to and fro, seeking whom he may devour. But if you are expectant and prepared, he can't devour you. This preparedness comes from putting on the whole armor of God. In doing so, we are truly only learning to walk in the victory Christ *already* won. And so we fight! We fight the good fight of faith as the apostle Paul declared he had done near the end of his life (1 Tim 6:12)! Because too much is at stake. We have too much to lose to do nothing! We must decide we are going to live for Christ, and in doing so, not only preserve our lives but make a difference in other lives because to decide to do nothing is to decide on nothing!

This fight, we learn, is not in man's strength but is mighty in God. It is not the power of man that's being used to fight this battle but God Himself. How could one using the weapons of God lose?

It is not possible. We could go on and on about the power of these weapons! The strongest weapons known to man could not compare to the power of God! All the armies of the earth could not compare!

In our opening, we referenced the book of Joel and God's warning for men to prepare for war. In fact, in Joel, we read they can take every piece of metal available and fashion it into a weapon, and it would not be enough to defeat God. Joel 3:10 declares emphatically, "Beat your plowshares into swords, and your pruning-hooks into spears." In other words, take everything available and turn it into a weapon to use. It will profit nothing, for God has won the battle. The results are just waiting to be played out as He has already dictated. And (while it will not be fully realized until Christ returns) we can already live in this victory!

Learn It!

This I can tell you has to happen if you are going to live the victorious life Christ died for believers to obtain—you *must* have your way of thinking transformed. Knowledge is foundational. Second Corinthians 10:4-5 declares, "For the weapons of our warfare are not carnal but mighty in God for the pulling down of strongholds, casting down arguments and every high thing that exalts itself *against the knowledge of God*, bringing every thought into captivity." We are armed against the enemy and prepared to walk in victory when we are armed with the knowledge of God. As we spoke about previously, Joshua won battles because he consulted with and believed what God told him he had was his. Scripture tells us Abraham received the child of promise because he hoped against all hope. He stood firm on the word of God and what God told him was for him. The battle starts in our mind, and our way of thinking to align with God's—accepting no less than what God through His words tells us we have and we are!

As we previously discussed, Isaiah 5:13 tells us, "My people have gone into captivity, because they have no knowledge." Furthermore, 2 Peter 1:2 says, "Grace and peace be multiplied unto you through the knowledge of God, and of Jesus our Lord." It is knowledge that is active in the life of a believer that can bring peace to our lives despite our circumstances. It's not merely knowledge of God but knowing God intimately. Don't miss this important point! It is the word of God infused in the believer of Christ empowered by the Holy Spirit that is the basis for obtaining the life Christ has planned for you!

Live It!

What we are promised here in 2 Corinthians 10 is a changed, victorious life for those who not only learn it but press in and live it— as they take every thought captive! But again, it is *not* in our power. Acts 5:32 tells us the Holy Spirit is given to those who are obedient to Christ. That is right—when you receive salvation, you are given the Holy Spirit so you can be successful. What God calls you to, He empowers you to do! This stands in stark contrast to those spoken of in 2 Timothy 3, which declares, "In the last days perilous times will come: For men will be lovers of themselves, lovers of money, boasters, proud, blasphemers, disobedient to parents, unthankful, unholy, unloving, unforgiving, slanderers, without self-control, brutal, despisers of good, traitors, headstrong, haughty, lovers of pleasure rather than lovers of God, having a form of godliness but denying its power." This group declares they are godly, but they deny and suppress and then do not truly have the relationship with Christ that leads to a changed life.

The ending of 2 Timothy 3 tells us though that, "All scripture is given by inspiration of God and is profitable for doctrine, for reproof, for correction, for instruction in righteousness, that the man of God may be complete, thoroughly equipped for every good work." It speaks to a different group who knows God and is transformed! The second group obtains the changed life we just read of 2 Corinthians 10:5-6 that instructs us to live what they have learned in Christ. It is in this that the battle is won—a changed life! It is a life that is grounded solidly in Christ—rooted in Him and built up in Him! We are called in Christ to be different. By His word we are equipped for every good work! After we are equipped, we must do! It is in this area that so many fall, we often know better but do less.

I recently attended a conference where John Maxwell spoke.[26] He said something I believe is very powerful in stating, "Many people have upward hopes but downward habits." Where do your habits, your actions take you—toward that upward calling or down the same destructive path the flesh always tends to like to go? Our faith is perfected when what we say we believe matches what we do. In the book of Hebrews, we read that there remains a rest for those in Christ, and we are warned not to fall like those in the Old Testament in the desert, who never entered the Promised Land (rest) because they were not obedient or did not live out what they professed they believed. Yes, their lack of obedience demonstrated truly their lack of total faith. Faith in action was essential!

---

[26] John Maxwell, *The One Thing to Get Right*. (Presented at the Global Leadership Summit, August 11-12, 2016).

Matthew 7:24–27 declares:

> Therefore whoever hears these sayings of Mine, and does them, I will liken him to a wise man who built his house on the rock: and the rain descended, the floods came, and the winds blew and beat on that house; and it did not fall, for it was founded on the rock. But everyone who hears these sayings of mine, and does not do them will be like a foolish man who built his house on the sand: and the rain descended, the floods came, and the winds blew and beat o that house; and it fell. And *great* was its fall.

The fall was so great because so much that could have been was lost! *Learn it **and** live it!*

It's *Not* Your Battle—the Battle Is Already Won, Promised, and Secured in Christ: Remain

I am reminded of the Israelites in the book of Nehemiah when they were allowed to go back to Jerusalem to rebuild the wall. The enemy did not leave them unopposed but did what he could to thwart, stop the building process. But God's people were instructed to fight. They were rebuilding the wall with a weapon in one hand and a tool in the other. Nevertheless, the wall was built as they pressed on and did not give in or up!

A scripture set I like to think on often in Hebrews 12:1–3, which tells us,

> Since we are surrounded by so great a cloud of witnesses, let us lay aside every weight, and the sin which so easily ensnares us, and let us run with endurance the race

> that is set before us, looking unto Jesus, the author and
> finisher of our faith, who for the joy set before endured
> the cross, despising the shame, and has sat down at the
> right hand of the throne of God.

In considering Paul fighting the good fight of faith, this scripture gives insight to his success—he kept his focus on Christ! Through all the many years imprisoned, the many beatings, through all the hardships and even to facing death at the end of his life, he was successful because he focused on Christ over the problem. We often don't have victory because we spend too much time focusing on the problem or the sin when we would have more freedom if we focused on Christ and accepted nothing less than what He tells us we have in Him!

Truly, all our hope, our victory, everything is in Christ above! Do you know Him? If you don't—turn to Him today and trust upon what He accomplished on the cross for your salvation! Maybe you know Christ as your Savior, but maybe you need to go deeper in your relationship with Him. Today you can make a decision to. Whatever battle you are facing, in Christ there is victory. Where the Spirit of the Lord is, there is liberty. And the Spirit of the Lord is built up in believers as they learn more of God and learn daily to simply trust in Him.

Free at Last!

I was thinking of that great *I Have a Dream* speech by Dr. Martin Luther King Jr.[27] He had a dream for people: for equality, for freedom!

---

[27] Dr. Martin Luther King Jr., "I Have a Dream Speech." 1963. https://www.archives.gov/files/press/exhibits/dream-speech.pdf

As he was a pastor who understood the gospel of Christ, I can assure you that Dr. King (while declaring a hope for a group of people in his speech) as a pastor also had hopes for all the people of God. The hope that they would understand and live in the understanding of the freedom they obtained when they received Christ as Savior. As a believer, you no longer have to believe the lie or live as if the lie has any power over you! (The lie being anything contrary to God's Word.)

Yes, it is sometimes a daily struggle, sometimes a minute-by-minute struggle to take every thought captive and to live the life Christ died for you to have—a life worthy of His sacrifice. But in Christ, as we are fully committed to and depending on Him—as we put on the whole armor of God—it is possible to be set free.

Along with Dr. King, I too share a dream—a dream for *all* the children of God to understand and to have—as the reality of their life and not just something simply hoped for—those timeless words King quoted as he recited the old hymn: *free at last, free at last, thank God almighty, I am free at last!*

Review/Application

1. Main Point(s): List what stood out to you:

2. What did you learn about:

    - yourself/human nature:

    - the enemy:

    - God:

3. What were the key scriptures that spoke to you and why?

4. How can you *practically* apply the principles in this chapter to your life?

49064768R00066

Made in the USA
Middletown, DE
05 October 2017